Table of Contents

1 Chapter 1: Understanding Criminal Conduct 3
1.1 Defining Criminal Behavior 7
1.2 Societal Impact of Crime 10
1.3 Root Causes of Offending 14

2 Chapter 2: Proactive Prevention Strategies 19
2.1 Community Engagement Initiatives 24
2.2 Early Intervention Programs 28

3 Chapter 3: Law Enforcement Effectiveness 33
3.1 Modern Policing Techniques 36
3.2 Intelligence Gathering and Analysis 41
3.3 Resource Allocation Strategies 45
3.4 Community Policing Models 48
3.5 Technological Advancements in Policing 52

4 Chapter 4: Judicial System Enhancements 57
4.1 Fair and Impartial Justice 61
4.2 Sentencing Guidelines and Reform 65

5 Chapter 5: Rehabilitation and Reintegration 71
5.1 Correctional Facility Reform 75
5.2 Vocational Training Programs 79
5.3 Support Systems for Ex-Offenders 84

6 Chapter 6: Addressing Specific Crime Types 89
6.1 Combating Violent Crime 93
6.2 Controlling Property Crime 97
6.3 Cybercrime Prevention and Response 100

7 Chapter 7: Maintaining Societal Stability 105
7.1 Building Trust in Institutions 110
7.2 Promoting Social Cohesion 114

1 Chapter 1: Understanding Criminal Conduct

Criminal conduct isn't a monolithic entity; it's a spectrum encompassing acts that violate established laws and norms. Defining it requires navigating a complex interplay of legal, social, and ethical considerations. Legally, a crime is an act or omission prohibited by law, punishable by sanctions like fines, imprisonment, or community service. But the law itself is a product of societal values and evolves over time. What was once considered acceptable, even commonplace, can become criminalized as a society's moral compass shifts. Consider historical examples like dueling, once a method of settling disputes among gentlemen, now illegal in most jurisdictions. Similarly, behaviors considered private matters, such as domestic violence, are increasingly recognized as crimes due to changing social attitudes. Therefore, a comprehensive definition of criminal behavior needs to consider the dynamic relationship between legal frameworks and societal expectations. Furthermore, cultural context plays a vital role. Actions deemed criminal in one society might be perfectly legal or even culturally sanctioned in another. Polygamy, for example, is criminalized in many Western countries but practiced legally in some parts of the world. These differences highlight the importance of understanding the specific cultural and legal landscape when analyzing criminal conduct. I think the challenge lies in creating laws that reflect shared values while respecting cultural diversity, ensuring that the definition of criminal behavior is both just and relevant across different contexts. This is where a nuanced approach that considers historical context, cultural variations, and the evolving nature of morality becomes essential for anyone seeking to understand the roots of crime and its potential remedies.

The reverberations of crime extend far beyond the immediate victim, impacting communities and the broader societal fabric in profound ways. Consider the economic costs. Crime drains resources from the economy through property damage, theft, and increased security measures. Businesses operating in high-crime areas often face higher insurance premiums, deterring investment and job creation. Government spending on law enforcement, the judicial system, and correctional facilities further diverts resources from essential services like education and healthcare. But the financial burden is only part of the story. The social impact of crime can be even more devastating. High crime rates erode trust within communities, creating an atmosphere of fear and suspicion. Residents may become reluctant to leave their homes, participate in community activities, or interact with their neighbors. This social isolation can weaken community bonds, making it harder to address local problems and fostering a cycle of decline. Think about the families of victims. The emotional trauma of crime can have long-lasting effects, leading to anxiety, depression, and post-traumatic stress disorder. Children who witness or experience violence are at increased risk of developing behavioral problems and engaging in criminal activity themselves. The cumulative effect of these individual tragedies can undermine the overall health and well-being of entire communities. Therefore, addressing crime requires a holistic approach that considers not only the legal consequences for offenders but also the needs of victims and the broader community. Investing in prevention programs, supporting victim services, and promoting community development are all essential steps in mitigating the societal impact of crime and restoring a sense of safety and security.

Unraveling the root causes of offending is a complex endeavor, involving a multifaceted examination of individual, social, and environmental factors. While there's no single explanation for criminal behavior, research suggests that a combination of influences often contribute to an individual's decision to engage in criminal activity. Poverty and socioeconomic inequality, for instance, can create environments where crime becomes a means of survival or a way to achieve social status. Limited access to education, employment opportunities, and healthcare can further exacerbate these conditions, leaving individuals feeling marginalized and disenfranchised. Social factors also play a significant role. Exposure to violence, either as a victim or a witness, can increase the likelihood of offending. Gang involvement, peer pressure, and dysfunctional family dynamics can also contribute to criminal behavior, particularly among young people. Furthermore, individual factors, such as mental health issues, substance abuse, and personality traits, can influence an individual's propensity to commit crimes. People with untreated mental illnesses may be more likely to engage in impulsive or violent behavior, while substance abuse can impair judgment and increase the risk of criminal activity. Early childhood experiences, such as neglect, abuse, or trauma, can also have lasting effects on brain development and emotional regulation, potentially increasing the risk of offending later in life. To effectively address the root causes of crime, a comprehensive approach is needed that targets both individual and societal factors. This includes investing in education, job training, and affordable housing, as well as providing access to mental health services and substance abuse treatment. Strengthening families, promoting positive peer relationships, and creating safe and supportive communities are also essential steps in preventing crime and fostering a more just and equitable society. By understanding the complex interplay of factors that contribute to criminal behavior, we can develop more effective strategies for preventing crime and creating a safer and more prosperous future for all. Moreover, it is important to promote positive role models and mentors, particularly for young people growing up in disadvantaged communities. These figures can provide guidance, support, and encouragement, helping young people navigate challenges and make positive choices.

1.1 Defining Criminal Behavior

Defining criminal behavior isn't as simple as pointing to a list of forbidden acts. It's a complex, multifaceted process shaped by history, culture, power, and evolving societal norms. What is considered a crime in one era or location might be perfectly acceptable, or even expected, in another. Consider, for example, historical laws regarding alcohol consumption or certain forms of labor. These once-criminalized behaviors are now commonplace, demonstrating the fluidity of the definition.

Criminal behavior, at its core, represents a violation of established laws and norms, carrying the potential for sanctions or penalties. The enforcement of these laws, however, is not always uniform. Factors such as social class, race, and geographic location can significantly influence how laws are applied and who is targeted. This disparity raises crucial questions about fairness, equity, and the potential for bias within the criminal justice system. Thinking about how these factors play out in real-world scenarios is essential for understanding the complexities of crime. We must acknowledge that the application of the law is not always neutral and objective, and the consequences of this reality can be profound.

To truly understand criminal behavior, one must venture beyond the legal definition and consider the context in which it occurs. A crucial aspect of understanding involves examining the intent behind an action. Was it premeditated, a crime of passion, or the result of negligence?

Understanding the motivations and circumstances surrounding a crime can provide valuable insights into the individual's behavior and inform appropriate responses. Moreover, it's vital to differentiate between mala in se and mala prohibita offenses. Mala in se refers to acts that are inherently wrong or evil, such as murder or theft. Mala prohibita, on the other hand, refers to acts that are wrong simply because they are prohibited by law, such as traffic violations or certain regulatory offenses. This distinction highlights how laws can be influenced by societal preferences and changing values.

Examining the interplay between individual actions and the broader social structure is also a critical step. Sociological perspectives emphasize the role of social inequality, poverty, and lack of opportunity in shaping criminal behavior. For instance, individuals living in impoverished communities may turn to crime as a means of survival due to limited economic prospects. Similarly, exposure to violence and criminal subcultures can normalize deviance and increase the likelihood of offending. These systemic factors can create a cycle of crime and disadvantage, making it difficult for individuals to escape. Therefore, effectively addressing criminal behavior requires tackling the root causes that contribute to it.

Psychological theories offer another layer of understanding, focusing on individual factors such as personality traits, cognitive processes, and emotional regulation. Some individuals may be predisposed to criminal behavior due to genetic factors or early childhood experiences. Others may lack empathy, exhibit impulsive tendencies, or have difficulty controlling their anger. These psychological factors can interact with environmental influences to increase the risk of offending. By understanding these individual vulnerabilities, interventions can be tailored to address specific needs and promote positive behavioral change. It involves understanding mental health issues, trauma, and other factors that might influence a person's choices.

Furthermore, it's important to recognize the dynamic nature of criminal behavior and the ways in which it evolves over time. Technological advancements, social trends, and policy changes can all influence the types of crimes that are committed and how they are addressed. For example, the rise of the internet has created new opportunities for cybercrime, such as hacking, identity theft, and online fraud. Similarly, changes in drug laws and attitudes towards substance use can impact the prevalence of drug-related offenses. Staying abreast of these evolving trends is essential for developing effective prevention and response strategies. We should regularly assess the impact of new technologies and social trends on criminal activities.

Consider the ethical dimensions. Criminal justice professionals, from law enforcement officers to judges to correctional officers, are entrusted with immense power. They must exercise this power responsibly and ethically, upholding the principles of fairness, impartiality, and due process. Ethical dilemmas are inherent in the system, requiring careful consideration of competing values and potential consequences. For instance, law enforcement officers must balance the need to protect public safety with the constitutional rights of individuals. Judges must ensure that sentences are just and proportionate to the crime. Correctional officers must maintain order and security while treating inmates with dignity and respect. Adherence to ethical standards is paramount to maintaining public trust and ensuring the integrity of the criminal justice system.

Finally, engaging in ongoing dialogue and critical reflection about criminal behavior is crucial for promoting positive change. This involves questioning assumptions, challenging biases, and seeking diverse perspectives. It also requires a commitment to evidence-based practices and a willingness to adapt strategies based on what works. By fostering a culture of continuous improvement, it is possible to create a more just, equitable, and effective criminal justice system. This requires input from experts, community members, and even those who have been involved in the system. Collaboration and open communication are essential for achieving meaningful progress. It is not solely the responsibility of law enforcement or government officials; it is a shared societal endeavor.

The task of defining criminal behavior is not an academic exercise; it is a fundamental prerequisite for creating a safer and more just society.

1.2 Societal Impact of Crime

Crime doesn't exist in a vacuum; it casts a long shadow, impacting every facet of our society. Its reach extends far beyond the immediate victims, permeating communities, economies, and even our collective sense of security. Understanding the breadth and depth of this impact is paramount to crafting effective strategies for its control. The cost of crime is multi-faceted, extending far beyond mere monetary values.

Consider the immediate impact on victims. Beyond the physical injuries and property loss, there's the often-unseen trauma, the psychological scars that can linger for years. Victims may experience anxiety, fear, depression, and post-traumatic stress disorder. The sense of safety and security is shattered, leading to a diminished quality of life. This ripple effect impacts their families and friends, who witness their loved one's suffering and grapple with their own anxieties. The emotional burden on victims and their support networks cannot be overstated, and it demands a compassionate and comprehensive response. Financial costs, while easier to quantify, are still substantial. These encompass medical expenses, property damage or loss, lost wages due to recovery, and the cost of therapy and counseling. Furthermore, victims may face legal fees if they pursue legal action against the perpetrator. These economic burdens can be particularly devastating for individuals and families already struggling financially, pushing them further into hardship.

The impact extends beyond the individual victim to entire communities. High crime rates can erode social cohesion, fostering distrust and fear among residents. People may become less likely to interact with their neighbors, participate in community events, or even venture out of their homes, particularly after dark. This social isolation can lead to a breakdown of community bonds, making it harder to address local issues and further exacerbating the problem of crime. Businesses, too, suffer in high-crime areas. They may face increased security costs, higher insurance premiums, and a decline in customers due to fear and safety concerns. Some businesses may even be forced to close down, leading to job losses and further economic decline in the community. The visible signs of crime, such as graffiti, vandalism, and abandoned properties, can also create a sense of neglect and decay, further demoralizing residents and deterring investment.

Economically, crime presents a significant drain on resources at every level, from local to national. Law enforcement agencies require funding for personnel, equipment, and training. The judicial system, including courts, prosecutors, and public defenders, incurs costs for trials, investigations, and legal proceedings. Correctional facilities demand substantial resources for housing, feeding, and supervising inmates. These costs are borne by taxpayers, diverting funds from other essential services such as education, healthcare, and infrastructure. Moreover, crime can deter tourism and investment, hindering economic growth and development. Businesses may be reluctant to locate in areas with high crime rates, and tourists may choose to visit safer destinations. This loss of economic activity can have a long-term negative impact on the community's prosperity and quality of life.

The pervasive fear of crime can also influence societal norms and behaviors. People may adopt self-protective measures, such as installing security systems, carrying weapons, or avoiding certain areas or activities. This can lead to a more guarded and less trusting society, where people are hesitant to interact with strangers or offer assistance to those in need. The constant awareness of crime can also contribute to a sense of anxiety and stress, impacting mental health and well-being. The media's portrayal of crime can further amplify these fears, even if the actual risk of victimization is relatively low. The constant exposure to stories of violence and crime can create a distorted perception of reality, leading to increased anxiety and a diminished sense of safety.

Addressing the societal impact of crime requires a multifaceted approach that goes beyond simply punishing offenders. It necessitates investing in prevention programs, supporting victims, strengthening communities, and reforming the criminal justice system. Early intervention programs targeting at-risk youth can help prevent them from becoming involved in crime in the first place. These programs can provide mentorship, education, and job training, helping young people develop the skills and opportunities they need to succeed. Supporting victims of crime is also crucial. This includes providing access to counseling, support groups, and financial assistance to help them recover from the trauma they have experienced. Strengthening communities by fostering social cohesion, promoting economic development, and improving access to resources can also help reduce crime rates. By investing in these areas, we can create safer, more resilient, and more prosperous communities for everyone.

Finally, criminal justice reform is essential to ensuring that the system is fair, just, and effective. This includes addressing issues such as racial bias, excessive sentencing, and the lack of rehabilitation programs in prisons. By reforming the criminal justice system, we can reduce recidivism rates, save taxpayer dollars, and create a more equitable society. Ultimately, addressing the societal impact of crime requires a collaborative effort involving individuals, communities, and government agencies. By working together, we can create a society where everyone feels safe, secure, and empowered to reach their full potential.

1.3 Root Causes of Offending

Understanding the roots of criminal offending is essential for crafting effective strategies that aim to reduce crime and promote societal well-being. It's a complex undertaking, diving into the multifaceted layers of human behavior, societal structures, and environmental influences. Ignoring these underlying causes is like treating the symptoms of an illness without addressing the disease itself; you might see temporary relief, but the problem will inevitably resurface.

One critical factor often overlooked is the cycle of poverty and lack of opportunity. When individuals lack access to education, job prospects, and basic resources, they may resort to criminal activity as a means of survival or to attain what seems unattainable through legitimate channels. It's not merely about material deprivation; it's about the absence of hope, the feeling of being trapped in a system that offers no way out. I've seen firsthand how providing access to vocational training and educational programs can break this cycle, offering individuals a pathway towards self-sufficiency and a sense of purpose. Consider, for example, a young person growing up in a neighborhood plagued by violence and unemployment. They may see drug dealing or gang involvement as their only viable option. However, if they are offered the opportunity to learn a trade, like carpentry or coding, and provided with mentorship and support, they may discover new aspirations and a different vision for their future. This doesn't excuse criminal behavior, but it helps to explain its origins and highlights the importance of addressing systemic inequalities.

Another significant contributor is the influence of dysfunctional family dynamics and adverse childhood experiences. Studies have consistently shown a strong correlation between childhood trauma, abuse, neglect, and future involvement in criminal activity. Children who grow up in environments marked by violence, substance abuse, or parental incarceration are more likely to experience emotional and behavioral problems that can lead to criminal behavior later in life. They may lack positive role models, struggle with emotional regulation, and develop distorted perceptions of the world around them. The impact of adverse childhood experiences can be profound and long-lasting. These experiences can disrupt brain development, impair social-emotional functioning, and increase the risk of mental health problems, all of which can contribute to criminal behavior. Early intervention programs, such as family therapy and trauma-informed care, are crucial for mitigating the effects of these experiences and helping children develop healthy coping mechanisms.

Furthermore, the role of social learning and peer influence cannot be understated. Individuals, especially during adolescence, are heavily influenced by their peers and the social norms of their environment. If someone is surrounded by individuals who engage in criminal behavior, they are more likely to adopt similar patterns of behavior themselves. This is not simply about conformity; it's about learning through observation and imitation. Young people may observe their peers engaging in criminal activities and perceive that there are no negative consequences, or even that there are social rewards, such as increased status or acceptance. Moreover, they may lack positive role models who can demonstrate alternative ways of behaving. Creating positive peer groups and providing opportunities for youth to engage in prosocial activities, such as sports, arts, or community service, can help to counteract these negative influences and promote positive social development.

Adding to this complex web are the underlying mental health issues. A significant portion of offenders struggle with untreated mental health conditions, such as depression, anxiety, bipolar disorder, or schizophrenia. These conditions can impair judgment, increase impulsivity, and contribute to violent behavior. Furthermore, individuals with mental health conditions may be more vulnerable to substance abuse, which can further exacerbate their symptoms and increase their risk of criminal involvement. It is essential to provide access to mental health services for offenders, both within correctional facilities and in the community. This includes screening for mental health conditions, providing individual and group therapy, and prescribing medication when appropriate.

The accessibility and misuse of substances is another crucial factor to consider. The connection between substance abuse and crime is well-established. Individuals under the influence of drugs or alcohol are more likely to engage in violent behavior, property crime, and other offenses. Furthermore, drug addiction can lead individuals to commit crimes in order to support their habit. Addressing substance abuse requires a comprehensive approach that includes prevention, treatment, and harm reduction strategies. Prevention efforts should focus on educating individuals about the risks of substance abuse and promoting healthy lifestyle choices. Treatment programs should provide evidence-based interventions, such as cognitive behavioral therapy and medication-assisted treatment. Harm reduction strategies, such as needle exchange programs and safe injection sites, can help to reduce the negative consequences of substance abuse.

Finally, the existing criminal justice system itself can, paradoxically, contribute to the problem. Overly punitive policies, such as mandatory minimum sentences and excessively long prison terms, can perpetuate a cycle of incarceration and make it more difficult for offenders to reintegrate into society after release. Moreover, the stigma associated with a criminal record can create significant barriers to employment, housing, and education, further increasing the risk of recidivism. A more restorative approach to justice, one that focuses on rehabilitation, reconciliation, and community restoration, is needed. This includes providing opportunities for offenders to make amends for their crimes, developing skills and competencies, and reconnecting with their communities.

In conclusion, there are no singular answers; multiple factors usually intertwine to generate criminal behavior. Understanding and addressing these root causes requires a holistic approach that involves collaboration between law enforcement, social services, educational institutions, and community organizations. By investing in prevention, early intervention, and rehabilitation programs, we can create safer, healthier, and more just communities for all. It is an ongoing process, requiring patience, persistence, and a commitment to addressing the underlying social and economic factors that contribute to crime.

2 Chapter 2: Proactive Prevention Strategies

Proactive prevention surpasses mere reaction; it embodies a strategic investment in community well-being, addressing the underlying factors that contribute to criminal behavior and aiming at stopping crime before it happens. It's about shifting the focus from solely punishing offenders to nurturing environments where crime is less likely to occur in the first place, thus emphasizing long-term stability and safety. This transformation demands a multi-faceted approach, intertwining community engagement with targeted early intervention programs, and demanding the active participation of residents, organizations, and law enforcement. Community engagement is not simply about holding town hall meetings; it's about fostering genuine, reciprocal relationships based on trust and mutual respect. One effective strategy is to establish neighborhood watch programs, empowering residents to become active participants in crime prevention. These programs not only increase surveillance and deter criminal activity, but also foster a sense of collective responsibility and shared ownership of community safety. Furthermore, community-led initiatives can address local needs and concerns, creating solutions that are tailored to the specific challenges faced by each neighborhood. For example, community gardens can provide safe spaces for residents to connect, build relationships, and access fresh produce, simultaneously combating food insecurity and promoting social cohesion. Similarly, local art projects can revitalize neglected areas, transforming them into vibrant public spaces that foster community pride and deter crime. I believe that successful community engagement requires sustained effort and a willingness to listen to and address the concerns of residents.

Early intervention programs represent a critical component of proactive prevention, targeting at-risk youth and providing them with the support and resources they need to thrive. These programs often focus on education, mentorship, and family support, addressing the root causes of delinquent behavior before they escalate into more serious offenses. One proven approach is to implement high-quality early childhood education programs, providing young children with a strong foundation for academic and social success. Research consistently demonstrates that children who participate in these programs are less likely to drop out of school, engage in criminal activity, and experience poverty later in life. In addition to educational interventions, mentorship programs can provide at-risk youth with positive role models and guidance, helping them navigate challenges and make informed decisions. These programs connect young people with adults who can provide support, encouragement, and a sense of belonging. My experience has shown that family support services play a vital role in preventing juvenile delinquency. These services can include parenting classes, family therapy, and access to resources that address issues such as poverty, substance abuse, and domestic violence. By strengthening families, early intervention programs can create stable and nurturing environments for children, reducing their risk of involvement in criminal activity.

To realize the full potential of proactive prevention, we must embrace a collaborative approach, recognizing that no single entity can address the problem of crime in isolation. Law enforcement agencies, community organizations, schools, families, and individual residents must work together, sharing information, coordinating resources, and supporting one another's efforts. This collaboration requires open communication, mutual respect, and a shared commitment to creating safer and more vibrant communities.

One way to foster collaboration is to establish community advisory boards, bringing together representatives from various stakeholder groups to identify local needs, develop strategies, and monitor progress. These boards can serve as a forum for dialogue, ensuring that all voices are heard and that decisions are made in a transparent and accountable manner. Furthermore, law enforcement agencies can partner with community organizations to provide training and resources to residents, empowering them to become active participants in crime prevention. For example, police officers can conduct workshops on home security, personal safety, and conflict resolution, equipping residents with the knowledge and skills they need to protect themselves and their communities.

Measuring the effectiveness of proactive prevention strategies is essential for ensuring that resources are being used wisely and that programs are achieving their intended outcomes. This requires collecting and analyzing data on crime rates, community engagement levels, and the impact of early intervention programs. It is crucial to use a variety of metrics, including both quantitative and qualitative data, to obtain a comprehensive understanding of the factors driving criminal behavior and the effectiveness of prevention efforts. Crime statistics can provide insights into trends and patterns, helping to identify areas where prevention efforts are most needed. Surveys and focus groups can gather information on community perceptions of safety, levels of trust in law enforcement, and the effectiveness of community engagement initiatives. And finally, program evaluations can assess the impact of early intervention programs on outcomes such as school attendance, academic achievement, and rates of juvenile delinquency. I know from years of experience that it's important to communicate the results of these evaluations to stakeholders, including residents, policymakers, and funders, to ensure that they are informed about the progress being made and that they can make informed decisions about resource allocation.

Investing in proactive prevention is not simply a matter of spending money; it's a strategic investment in the long-term health and well-being of our communities. While these strategies may require upfront funding, they have the potential to generate significant cost savings in the long run by reducing the need for reactive measures such as law enforcement, incarceration, and victim services. Furthermore, proactive prevention can create safer, more vibrant communities that attract residents, businesses, and investment, leading to economic growth and improved quality of life. Let me say that implementing proactive prevention strategies requires a long-term commitment and a willingness to adapt and innovate. There is no one-size-fits-all approach, and what works in one community may not work in another. Therefore, it is essential to continuously evaluate the effectiveness of prevention efforts and to make adjustments as needed based on the data and feedback collected. This requires a culture of continuous improvement, where stakeholders are willing to learn from their mistakes, share best practices, and embrace new approaches. Moreover, sustained funding is crucial for ensuring the long-term success of proactive prevention efforts. Prevention programs often require significant upfront investment, and they may not yield immediate results. Therefore, it is essential to secure stable and reliable funding sources, such as government grants, private foundations, and community fundraising, to ensure that these programs can continue to operate effectively over time. In the end, proactive prevention is not a quick fix, but a long-term strategy for building safer, healthier, and more resilient communities. It requires a commitment to addressing the underlying causes of crime, fostering collaboration, and investing in the well-being of our young people. By embracing this approach, we can create communities where everyone has the opportunity to thrive, and where crime is no longer a barrier to progress and prosperity.

2.1 Community Engagement Initiatives

Community engagement is not just a feel-good add-on to criminal element control; it's a foundational pillar. Think of it as cultivating a garden: you can't just pull weeds (react to crime) and expect it to flourish. You need to nourish the soil, plant the right seeds (positive community initiatives), and tend to it regularly. This chapter dives into practical, actionable initiatives that transform communities from breeding grounds for crime into vibrant, self-policing environments. We're talking about going beyond the occasional neighborhood watch meeting and implementing strategies that address the root causes of criminal behavior while fostering a sense of collective responsibility.

One crucial aspect often overlooked is creating opportunities for meaningful dialogue. It's not enough for police to simply patrol neighborhoods; they need to actively engage with residents in non-enforcement settings. Picture this: a "Coffee with a Cop" event held at a local community center. These informal gatherings allow residents to voice concerns, share information, and build relationships with law enforcement officers in a relaxed, non-threatening atmosphere. The key here is authenticity and genuine listening. Officers should be trained to actively listen, empathize with residents' experiences, and respond in a transparent and accountable manner. These interactions dismantle barriers, foster trust, and empower residents to become active partners in crime prevention. Furthermore, consider town hall meetings focused on specific issues, such as youth violence or drug activity. These forums provide a platform for community members, law enforcement, local government officials, and community leaders to collectively brainstorm solutions and develop action plans. The success of these initiatives hinges on ensuring diverse representation from all segments of the community, including marginalized groups whose voices are often unheard. The most effective dialogues are those that translate into tangible actions, demonstrating that community concerns are being taken seriously.

Another impactful initiative is investing in youth empowerment programs. Crime often stems from a lack of opportunity and positive role models. Creating safe spaces and providing resources for young people can significantly reduce their involvement in criminal activity. Imagine after-school programs offering tutoring, mentoring, and recreational activities. These programs not only provide academic support but also expose youth to positive influences and alternative pathways to success. Consider partnering with local businesses and organizations to offer vocational training and job placement opportunities for young adults. Equipping youth with marketable skills and connecting them to employment can break the cycle of poverty and reduce the allure of criminal activity. Sports leagues, arts programs, and community service projects are also valuable tools for engaging youth and fostering a sense of belonging. These activities provide positive outlets for energy, build teamwork skills, and instill a sense of civic responsibility. The key is to create programs that are youth-led and responsive to their needs and interests, ensuring that they are actively involved in shaping their own futures.

Furthermore, addressing environmental factors can have a profound impact on crime rates. The "broken windows" theory suggests that visible signs of neglect and disorder, such as graffiti, abandoned buildings, and litter, can create an environment that encourages more serious crime. Implementing community beautification projects can transform blighted areas into vibrant, welcoming spaces. Imagine residents coming together to clean up parks, plant trees, and paint murals. These efforts not only improve the physical appearance of the neighborhood but also foster a sense of pride and ownership, discouraging criminal activity. Improving street lighting, installing security cameras, and implementing neighborhood watch programs can also enhance safety and deter crime. These measures create a sense of collective surveillance, making it more difficult for criminals to operate undetected. The effectiveness of these initiatives hinges on collaboration between residents, local government, and law enforcement. Residents should be empowered to identify problem areas and participate in developing solutions. Local government should provide resources and support for community-led initiatives. Law enforcement should work closely with residents to address crime hotspots and implement targeted interventions.

Restorative justice practices offer a powerful alternative to traditional punitive approaches. These practices focus on repairing harm, holding offenders accountable, and reintegrating them back into the community. Imagine a victim-offender mediation program where victims have the opportunity to confront their offenders, share their experiences, and participate in developing a plan for repairing the harm caused by the crime. These programs can provide closure for victims, promote empathy among offenders, and reduce recidivism rates. Community service projects, where offenders contribute to the well-being of the community, can also be a powerful form of restorative justice. These projects not only hold offenders accountable for their actions but also provide them with an opportunity to give back to the community and make amends for their wrongdoing. The success of restorative justice practices hinges on ensuring that they are voluntary, safe, and equitable. Victims should be fully informed about their rights and options, and offenders should be held accountable in a way that is both just and restorative.

Finally, sustained and transparent communication is essential for building trust and maintaining community engagement. Create a community newsletter to share information about crime trends, community events, and upcoming initiatives. Utilize social media platforms to connect with residents, share updates, and solicit feedback. Host regular community meetings to discuss issues of concern and brainstorm solutions. The key is to create multiple channels for communication and ensure that information is accessible to all residents. Remember, community engagement is not a one-time event but an ongoing process. It requires sustained effort, genuine commitment, and a willingness to listen to and learn from the community. By investing in these initiatives, we can transform communities from breeding grounds for crime into vibrant, self-policing environments where everyone feels safe, valued, and empowered.

2.2 Early Intervention Programs

Early intervention programs are not just feel-good initiatives; they are strategic investments in the future well-being of communities and the reduction of criminal behavior. These programs target individuals, often children and adolescents, who are identified as being at risk of engaging in criminal activity later in life. The goal is to address underlying issues – poverty, family dysfunction, educational deficits, exposure to violence – that significantly increase the likelihood of future offending. Success hinges on identifying these at-risk individuals early and providing them with the resources and support they need to navigate potential pitfalls and develop into law-abiding, productive members of society.

The key to effective early intervention lies in a multi-faceted approach. One size rarely fits all. Programs should be tailored to the specific needs of the target population, taking into account factors such as age, gender, cultural background, and the nature of the risks they face. A comprehensive approach often involves a combination of academic support, mentoring, family therapy, and skill-building activities. For example, a program designed to prevent gang involvement might offer tutoring to improve academic performance, conflict resolution training to teach alternative ways of resolving disputes, and vocational training to provide viable employment options. Crucially, these programs must be delivered by qualified professionals who are trained to work with at-risk youth and who are sensitive to the unique challenges they face.

Family involvement is a critical component of successful early intervention programs. Children are heavily influenced by their home environment, and interventions that neglect the family are unlikely to achieve lasting results. Programs should actively engage parents or guardians, providing them with the tools and support they need to create a stable and nurturing home environment. This might include parenting classes, family therapy, and assistance with accessing essential resources such as housing, food, and healthcare. By strengthening families, we can create a protective buffer against the risk factors that contribute to criminal behavior.

Education plays a pivotal role. Many at-risk youth struggle academically, which can lead to frustration, disengagement, and ultimately, dropping out of school. Early intervention programs should prioritize educational support, providing tutoring, mentoring, and other resources to help students succeed in the classroom. This also includes addressing issues such as bullying, truancy, and school discipline policies that can disproportionately affect at-risk youth. Furthermore, programs should promote access to quality early childhood education, which has been shown to have a significant positive impact on long-term academic and social outcomes. Investing in education is an investment in a brighter future, reducing the likelihood of involvement in the criminal justice system.

Mental health services are vital, often overlooked. Many at-risk youth experience mental health issues such as anxiety, depression, and post-traumatic stress disorder. These issues can significantly increase the risk of criminal behavior, as individuals may turn to drugs or violence as a way to cope with their pain. Early intervention programs should provide access to mental health services, including counseling, therapy, and medication management. Addressing mental health needs can not only improve the individual's well-being but also reduce the likelihood of future offending. Removing the barriers to mental health care is crucial to preventing crime before it occurs.

Community partnerships are essential for the success of early intervention programs. These programs cannot operate in isolation. They need to work closely with schools, law enforcement agencies, social service organizations, and other community stakeholders to identify at-risk youth and provide them with the support they need. Community partnerships can also help to raise awareness about the importance of early intervention and mobilize resources to support these programs. By working together, communities can create a network of support that helps at-risk youth stay on the right path.

Measuring the effectiveness of early intervention programs is critical to ensuring that they are achieving their intended goals. Programs should be regularly evaluated to assess their impact on outcomes such as academic achievement, behavior problems, and involvement in the criminal justice system. These evaluations should use rigorous research methods and should take into account factors such as program fidelity and participant characteristics. By measuring the effectiveness of programs, we can identify what works and what doesn't, and we can make adjustments to improve their impact. The use of evidence-based practices and continuous improvement are key to maximizing the return on investment in early intervention.

Ultimately, early intervention programs are an investment in prevention. They are a proactive approach to reducing crime and building safer, more resilient communities. While they require an upfront investment of resources, they can save significant costs in the long run by reducing the need for law enforcement, courts, and correctional facilities. More importantly, they can improve the lives of at-risk youth, giving them the opportunity to reach their full potential and contribute positively to society. By investing in early intervention, we can create a future where fewer young people become involved in the criminal justice system and where all members of our communities have the opportunity to thrive.

3 Chapter 3: Law Enforcement Effectiveness

Law enforcement effectiveness hinges on a multifaceted approach, one that moves beyond reactive responses to proactive, intelligence-driven strategies. Modern policing is not simply about patrolling streets; it's about understanding the complex interplay of factors that contribute to crime and deploying resources in the most effective manner to address those factors. This involves a deep understanding of crime statistics, demographics, and social conditions within a community, coupled with the ability to analyze data and predict potential hotspots.

A critical component of modern policing revolves around intelligence gathering and analysis. It's no longer sufficient to simply respond to crimes after they occur. Agencies must proactively gather information about potential threats, identify criminal networks, and understand the underlying motivations behind criminal activity. This requires a sophisticated intelligence apparatus capable of collecting, analyzing, and disseminating information to officers in the field. Sources of intelligence are varied, ranging from traditional informants and undercover operations to the utilization of advanced surveillance technologies and data mining techniques. Consider the impact of predictive policing, utilizing algorithms to analyze historical crime data to forecast areas and times with a higher likelihood of criminal activity. This allows for the strategic deployment of resources to deter crime before it happens, focusing on prevention rather than simply response. Such strategies are not without controversy, however. Concerns about bias in data and the potential for discriminatory targeting must be carefully addressed through rigorous oversight and ethical guidelines.

Resource allocation is another crucial aspect of law enforcement effectiveness. Simply having a large number of officers is not enough. Resources must be deployed strategically, based on data and analysis, to maximize their impact. This may involve shifting resources from low-crime areas to high-crime areas, or focusing on specific types of crime that are particularly problematic. Specialized units, such as gang task forces or drug enforcement units, can be highly effective in addressing specific types of criminal activity. However, it's essential to ensure that these units are properly trained and supervised, and that they operate in a way that is consistent with community values. We must continually evaluate resource allocation strategies to ensure that they are achieving their intended goals. This involves tracking crime statistics, monitoring officer activity, and soliciting feedback from the community. The effectiveness of different strategies will vary depending on the specific context of each community. There is no one-size-fits-all solution.

Community policing models represent a significant shift away from traditional law enforcement approaches. Instead of simply focusing on arresting criminals, community policing emphasizes building relationships with residents, businesses, and community organizations. This involves officers becoming more involved in the community, attending community meetings, and working with residents to identify and solve problems. The goal is to create a sense of partnership between the police and the community, where residents feel comfortable reporting crime and working with officers to address issues of concern. This approach can be particularly effective in reducing crime in areas where trust between the police and the community is low. By building relationships and fostering a sense of shared responsibility, community policing can create a more positive and collaborative environment for addressing crime.

Technological advancements are rapidly transforming the landscape of policing. Body-worn cameras, for example, are becoming increasingly common, providing a record of interactions between officers and the public. This can help to increase transparency and accountability, as well as provide valuable evidence in criminal investigations. Automated license plate readers (ALPRs) can be used to track vehicles associated with criminal activity, while facial recognition technology can be used to identify suspects. However, the use of these technologies raises important ethical and legal questions about privacy and civil liberties. It's crucial to develop clear policies and regulations governing the use of these technologies to ensure that they are used responsibly and ethically. Data security and the potential for misuse must be carefully considered.

Ultimately, law enforcement effectiveness is not simply about arresting more people or solving more crimes. It's about creating safer and more resilient communities. This requires a holistic approach that addresses the underlying causes of crime, builds trust between the police and the community, and utilizes resources strategically and ethically. It requires a commitment to continuous improvement, a willingness to adapt to changing circumstances, and a deep understanding of the complex factors that contribute to crime. A successful strategy also incorporates a deep appreciation of the social context in which crime occurs.

3.1 Modern Policing Techniques

Modern policing is no longer solely about responding to crime after it occurs; it's about anticipating, preventing, and addressing the root causes. This evolution demands a multifaceted approach, leveraging technology, community partnerships, and data-driven strategies. The traditional image of a police officer simply patrolling streets is being replaced by a more nuanced and sophisticated role. To maintain societal calm and stability, law enforcement agencies must adapt and embrace these changes, moving beyond reactive responses to proactive problem-solving.

Consider the use of predictive policing. This technique involves analyzing crime data to identify patterns and predict future offenses. By focusing resources on high-risk areas and times, police can deter crime before it happens. For instance, imagine a city experiencing a spike in burglaries in a particular neighborhood. By analyzing the data, police can identify factors contributing to the trend, such as poorly lit streets or vacant properties. They can then increase patrols in those areas, improve street lighting, and work with property owners to secure vacant buildings. This targeted approach is far more effective than simply increasing patrols across the entire city. Predictive policing isn't about profiling individuals, but rather about understanding patterns and allocating resources strategically. However, it requires careful implementation to avoid bias and ensure fairness. Data used for prediction should be continuously monitored and evaluated to prevent perpetuating existing disparities.

Data-driven policing extends beyond predictive analysis, encompassing a broader range of applications. CompStat, for example, is a management philosophy that uses crime data to hold commanders accountable for reducing crime in their precincts. Regular CompStat meetings provide a forum for reviewing crime statistics, identifying problems, and developing strategies for addressing them. This approach fosters a culture of accountability and encourages innovation in crime fighting. Another valuable tool is crime mapping, which allows police to visualize crime patterns and identify hotspots. This information can be used to deploy resources more effectively and target specific crime problems. For example, if a city is experiencing a rise in car thefts near public transportation hubs, police can increase patrols in those areas and work with transit authorities to improve security measures. The key to successful data-driven policing is ensuring that the data is accurate, reliable, and used ethically. Police departments must also invest in training officers to analyze data and use it to inform their decisions.

Community policing remains a cornerstone of modern law enforcement. Building trust and rapport with residents is essential for gathering information, solving crimes, and preventing future offenses. Community policing involves assigning officers to specific neighborhoods and encouraging them to build relationships with residents, business owners, and community leaders. These officers become familiar with the unique challenges and needs of their assigned areas. This allows them to tailor their approach to address local concerns and build stronger relationships with the community. The emphasis on collaboration and problem-solving is different from traditional reactive policing. Community policing strategies can include foot patrols, neighborhood meetings, and community events. Officers can also work with residents to identify and address issues such as blight, drug dealing, and gang activity. When police and community members work together, they can create safer and more vibrant neighborhoods.

Technological advancements are revolutionizing policing. Body-worn cameras provide a valuable tool for accountability and transparency, capturing interactions between officers and the public. The use of drones can assist in search and rescue operations, crime scene investigations, and surveillance. License plate readers can help identify stolen vehicles and track down suspects. Social media can be used to gather information, communicate with the public, and disseminate crime prevention tips. It's worth adding that technology is merely a tool, and its effectiveness depends on how it is used. For example, body-worn cameras can improve accountability, but they must be used in accordance with clear policies and procedures. License plate readers can help solve crimes, but they must be used in a way that respects privacy rights. Implementing such technology requires careful consideration of its potential impact on civil liberties.

The shift towards problem-oriented policing reflects a move away from reactive responses to proactive solutions. Problem-oriented policing involves identifying specific crime problems, analyzing their underlying causes, and developing targeted strategies for addressing them. For instance, imagine a city experiencing a high number of robberies at convenience stores. Instead of simply increasing patrols in the area, police might analyze the factors contributing to the problem. They might discover that many of the robberies occur late at night when stores are understaffed and poorly lit. Based on this analysis, they can work with store owners to improve security measures, such as installing brighter lighting, increasing staffing levels, and implementing robbery prevention training for employees. This problem-solving approach addresses the root causes of the crime and is likely to be more effective than simply increasing patrols. Problem-oriented policing requires officers to be creative, resourceful, and collaborative. They must work with community members, businesses, and other government agencies to identify and address the underlying causes of crime.

Moving beyond traditional methods also means focusing on de-escalation techniques. De-escalation training equips officers with the skills to resolve conflicts peacefully, reducing the likelihood of violence. This training emphasizes communication skills, empathy, and the ability to assess situations and make informed decisions. Officers learn how to recognize signs of distress, listen actively, and use verbal and nonverbal techniques to calm individuals down. They are also taught to use less-lethal force options when appropriate. De-escalation training is essential for improving police-community relations and reducing the number of use-of-force incidents. It requires a commitment from police departments to provide ongoing training and support to officers. By prioritizing de-escalation, police can build trust with the community and create a safer environment for everyone.

Finally, modern policing embraces evidence-based practices. This means relying on research and data to inform decisions and evaluate the effectiveness of policing strategies. Before implementing a new program or policy, police departments should review the available research to determine whether it is likely to be effective. They should also collect data to evaluate the impact of their initiatives. Evidence-based policing helps ensure that resources are being used effectively and that policing strategies are having the desired impact. It requires a commitment to continuous learning and improvement. Police departments must be willing to experiment with new approaches and to evaluate their effectiveness. By embracing evidence-based practices, police can improve their effectiveness and build trust with the community.

3.2 Intelligence Gathering and Analysis

Intelligence gathering and analysis form the backbone of any effective strategy to prevent criminal conduct. This is where we transition from simply reacting to crimes to proactively understanding and anticipating them, thereby allowing us to get ahead of the curve, but where do we start? It starts with understanding that intelligence is not just about collecting information, it's about transforming that information into actionable insight.

The first step is defining your intelligence requirements. What specific criminal activities are you trying to address? What information do you need to understand the individuals or groups involved? Are you trying to discern patterns, predict future actions, or identify vulnerabilities? The clearer your requirements, the more focused and effective your intelligence gathering efforts will be. Think of it like building a house; you wouldn't start hammering nails without a blueprint, would you? Similarly, don't start collecting data without a clear idea of what you are looking for. Prioritization here is key. You will quickly find that there is an overwhelming amount of information available, but not all of it is relevant or useful. Focus your efforts on the most critical intelligence gaps, the pieces of information that will have the biggest impact on your ability to prevent or disrupt criminal activity.

Once you have defined your requirements, it's time to consider your sources. Information can come from a wide range of places, both overt and covert. Law enforcement databases, incident reports, and court records are valuable sources of public information. Community informants, neighborhood watch groups, and even social media can provide valuable tips and insights, but this is a delicate dance. You must balance the need for information with the need to protect privacy and civil liberties. Consider, for example, the information available on social media. While it can be a goldmine of information about individuals and groups, it's also important to remember that people often present a curated version of themselves online. Verify information from multiple sources before drawing any conclusions.

Collection methodologies are crucial. How will you gather the information you need? Surveillance, interviews, and undercover operations are some of the more traditional methods, but they can be resource-intensive and potentially risky. There are some more creative ideas to ponder here. Could you partner with local businesses to gather information on suspicious activity? Could you use data analytics to identify patterns in crime reports? The key is to be adaptable and think outside the box, but always within the confines of the law. Make sure you have the legal authority to collect the information you are seeking, and that you are following proper procedures to protect privacy and ensure the integrity of the evidence.

Analysis is where the real magic happens. Gathering information is only half the battle, you must transform it into something useful. This involves organizing the data, identifying patterns and trends, and drawing conclusions about the nature and scope of the criminal activity you are investigating. Tools like link analysis software can help you visualize relationships between individuals, organizations, and events, revealing hidden connections that might otherwise go unnoticed. Don't be afraid to look for the "so what?" What does this information mean? How does it affect our understanding of the problem? What actions should we take as a result?

Dissemination is about getting the right information to the right people at the right time. It's no good gathering all this intelligence if it just sits in a report on your desk. Think about who needs to know what, and how you can best communicate the information to them. Should you send a formal report to your superiors? Should you share the information with other law enforcement agencies? Should you brief community leaders on the latest trends in criminal activity? Consider the sensitivity of the information and take steps to protect it from unauthorized disclosure. Remember, the goal is to inform decision-making and facilitate action.

Finally, remember that intelligence gathering and analysis is an ongoing process. The criminal landscape is constantly evolving, and you must adapt your strategies accordingly. Regularly evaluate the effectiveness of your intelligence efforts. Are you gathering the right information? Are you analyzing it effectively? Are you getting it to the people who need it? Be willing to make changes as needed to stay one step ahead of the criminal element. Conduct after-action reviews of successful and unsuccessful operations to identify lessons learned. Share best practices with other agencies and organizations. The more you invest in your intelligence capabilities, the better equipped you will be to protect your community and maintain societal calm and stability.

I've found that one of the biggest mistakes organizations make is failing to prioritize analytical training. Simply providing access to sophisticated software isn't enough. Analysts need to be trained in critical thinking, data analysis techniques, and effective communication. They need to understand how to identify biases, evaluate sources, and draw sound conclusions from incomplete or conflicting information. Invest in your people, and they will provide you with the insights you need to make informed decisions.

Also, remember ethical considerations. Intelligence gathering and analysis can raise significant ethical concerns, particularly around privacy and civil liberties. You must develop clear policies and procedures to ensure that intelligence activities are conducted in a lawful and ethical manner. Be transparent about your intelligence activities, and be willing to be held accountable for your actions. Remember that your goal is to protect the community, not to infringe on the rights of its members. Building and maintaining public trust is essential for the long-term success of any crime prevention strategy.

In a complex, rapidly changing world, intelligence gathering and analysis are more important than ever. By investing in your intelligence capabilities, you can gain a deeper understanding of criminal activity, develop more effective prevention strategies, and build a safer, more stable society. Don't underestimate the power of information. Used wisely, it can be your most potent weapon in the fight against crime.

3.3 Resource Allocation Strategies

Resource Allocation Strategies

Effective resource allocation is the cornerstone of any successful law enforcement agency striving to maintain societal calm. It's not simply about having enough officers or equipment; it's about strategically deploying these assets to maximize their impact on crime reduction and community safety. Poor allocation can leave communities vulnerable, waste valuable resources, and ultimately undermine public trust, so that we can reduce risks associated with safety.

The first step in any effective resource allocation strategy is a thorough assessment of the jurisdiction's crime landscape. This involves analyzing crime statistics, identifying hotspots, understanding crime trends, and assessing the specific needs of different communities. I recommend paying close attention to the types of crimes occurring, their frequency, the times and locations they occur, and any patterns or correlations that emerge. Data-driven approaches are invaluable here; use crime mapping software, statistical analysis tools, and predictive policing models to gain a comprehensive understanding of the challenges you face. Furthermore, don't rely solely on official crime statistics; supplement this data with community surveys, feedback from officers on the ground, and information from partner agencies to get a more holistic picture. It is clear, therefore, that efficient resourcing is very important.

Once you have a clear understanding of the crime landscape, the next step is to prioritize your resources based on the areas of greatest need. This might involve focusing on high-crime areas, addressing specific types of crime that are particularly prevalent, or targeting repeat offenders. Remember that prioritization should be evidence-based and data-driven, not based on political pressure or anecdotal evidence. I suggest developing clear and measurable objectives for each priority area and allocating resources accordingly. For example, if you're targeting drug-related crime in a particular neighborhood, you might allocate additional patrol officers, specialized drug enforcement units, and community outreach programs to that area. Regularly evaluate the effectiveness of your resource allocation decisions and make adjustments as needed based on the results you're achieving.

Beyond simply assigning personnel to specific areas, consider implementing specialized units to address particular crime types or community needs. These might include gang units, domestic violence units, traffic enforcement units, or community policing teams. Specialized units allow officers to develop expertise in specific areas, improving their effectiveness and allowing them to build strong relationships with the communities they serve. However, it's crucial to ensure that these units are properly staffed and supported, and that their activities are coordinated with other law enforcement efforts. Overlapping mandates or conflicting priorities can undermine the effectiveness of specialized units and create confusion among officers.

Community policing models are another vital component of effective resource allocation. Community policing emphasizes building strong relationships between law enforcement officers and the communities they serve, fostering trust and cooperation. This can be achieved through foot patrols, neighborhood meetings, community events, and other initiatives that bring officers into closer contact with residents. I have seen that community policing can be incredibly effective in reducing crime and improving public safety, but it requires a significant investment of resources. It's not simply about assigning officers to walk a beat; it's about providing them with the training, support, and time they need to build genuine relationships with community members.

Technology can play a powerful role in enhancing resource allocation. Consider using real-time crime mapping software to track crime incidents as they occur and deploy officers to where they are needed most. Body-worn cameras can provide valuable evidence in criminal investigations and promote accountability. Data analytics tools can help you identify crime patterns and trends, allowing you to anticipate and prevent crime before it occurs. Be aware that technology is not a substitute for human interaction; it should be used to augment, not replace, traditional policing methods. Also, be mindful of privacy concerns and ensure that you are using technology responsibly and ethically.

A frequently overlooked aspect of resource allocation is officer wellness. Stress, burnout, and fatigue can significantly impair an officer's ability to perform their duties effectively. Make sure your officers have access to adequate support services, including counseling, stress management training, and peer support programs. Encourage them to take time off to rest and recharge, and promote a healthy work-life balance. A well-rested, supported officer is a more effective officer, and investing in officer wellness is an investment in community safety.

Lastly, resource allocation is not a static process; it needs to be continuously evaluated and adjusted based on changing circumstances. Regularly review your data, solicit feedback from officers and community members, and assess the effectiveness of your strategies. Be willing to experiment with new approaches and adapt your tactics as needed. The key is to be flexible, responsive, and data-driven in your resource allocation decisions. Also, consider external factors like economic downturns or social unrest, which can impact crime rates and require adjustments to your resource allocation plans. By embracing a continuous improvement approach, you can ensure that your resources are being used effectively to protect your community and maintain societal calm.

3.4 Community Policing Models

Community policing represents a significant departure from traditional, reactive law enforcement models. Instead of solely responding to calls for service and focusing on arrests, community policing prioritizes building relationships with residents, addressing the root causes of crime, and fostering collaborative problem-solving. It's about embedding officers within neighborhoods, making them accessible and accountable, and empowering communities to take an active role in their own safety. This model acknowledges that law enforcement alone cannot solve crime problems effectively; true solutions require a partnership between police and the people they serve.

One of the core tenets of community policing is decentralization. Rather than operating solely from centralized police stations, community policing encourages officers to establish a visible presence in specific neighborhoods. This might involve foot patrols, bicycle patrols, or even establishing community substations within residential areas. The goal is to create opportunities for informal interaction between officers and residents, allowing them to get to know each other on a personal level. This increased visibility also serves as a deterrent to crime, as offenders are less likely to commit offenses in areas where police presence is consistent and visible. Furthermore, by being readily available within the community, officers can respond more quickly and effectively to emerging problems and address residents' concerns directly.

Problem-oriented policing is another crucial component, shifting the focus from simply responding to individual incidents to identifying and addressing the underlying issues that contribute to crime. This involves conducting thorough analyses of crime data to identify patterns and hotspots, as well as engaging with residents to understand their perceptions of crime problems and potential solutions. For example, instead of simply responding to repeated calls about noise complaints at a particular apartment building, officers might work with the landlord and tenants to address the underlying causes of the noise, such as inadequate soundproofing or disruptive residents. This proactive approach can lead to more sustainable solutions than simply responding to individual complaints.

Collaboration and partnerships are essential to the success of these efforts. Law enforcement agencies cannot operate in isolation; they must work collaboratively with a wide range of stakeholders, including residents, community organizations, businesses, schools, and other government agencies. These partnerships can take many forms, from community meetings and neighborhood watch programs to joint initiatives targeting specific crime problems. By pooling resources and expertise, these partnerships can develop more comprehensive and effective solutions than any single entity could achieve alone. For instance, a partnership between police, schools, and social service agencies might focus on providing at-risk youth with mentoring, tutoring, and other support services to prevent them from becoming involved in criminal activity.

Training and education are also vital for the successful implementation of such models. Officers need to be trained not only in traditional law enforcement skills but also in communication, conflict resolution, and community engagement. They need to understand the importance of building relationships with residents, actively listening to their concerns, and treating them with respect, regardless of their background or socioeconomic status. This requires a shift in mindset from being simply enforcers of the law to being problem-solvers and partners with the community. It also requires ongoing training and support to ensure that officers have the skills and knowledge they need to effectively implement these strategies.

Measuring success in community policing requires a different approach than traditional law enforcement metrics. Instead of solely focusing on arrest rates and crime statistics, it is important to also measure community satisfaction, trust in police, and the overall quality of life in the community. These measures can provide a more comprehensive picture of the effectiveness of community policing strategies and help to identify areas for improvement. For example, surveys can be used to gauge residents' perceptions of safety and their satisfaction with police services. Community meetings can provide a forum for residents to voice their concerns and provide feedback on police performance. By regularly assessing these measures, law enforcement agencies can ensure that their community policing efforts are truly making a difference.

Challenges and obstacles must be acknowledged. One common challenge is resistance from within the law enforcement agency itself. Some officers may be skeptical of these models, viewing them as "soft on crime" or believing that they are not "real police work." Overcoming this resistance requires strong leadership, clear communication about the benefits of community policing, and ongoing training and support for officers. Another challenge is building trust with communities that have historically had negative experiences with law enforcement. This requires sustained effort to demonstrate a commitment to fairness, transparency, and accountability. It also requires actively engaging with community leaders and residents to address their concerns and build relationships based on mutual respect.

Furthermore, resources constraints are frequently a stumbling block. Implementing effective programs requires adequate funding for training, personnel, and equipment. Law enforcement agencies may need to reallocate resources to support these efforts, or they may need to seek additional funding from government or private sources. Finally, sustaining community policing efforts over time can be difficult, particularly when faced with competing priorities or changes in leadership. It is important to institutionalize these models by embedding them into the agency's policies, procedures, and culture. This ensures that community policing remains a priority, even when faced with challenges or changes in leadership. It's a marathon, not a sprint, a way of doing things, not merely a program that can be easily shelved.

3.5 Technological Advancements in Policing

Policing has undergone a dramatic transformation in recent decades, largely fueled by leaps in technological innovation. These advancements offer unparalleled opportunities to enhance crime prevention, improve response times, and strengthen evidence collection. However, the implementation of these technologies also presents complex ethical and prac-

tical considerations that must be carefully addressed. One of the most transformative developments has been the widespread adoption of body-worn cameras (BWCs). These devices record interactions between officers and the public, providing a visual and audio record of events. The benefits are multifold: enhanced transparency and accountability, reduced instances of misconduct allegations, and a more accurate record of events for investigative purposes. Moreover, studies have shown that BWCs can lead to a decrease in both citizen complaints and uses of force by officers. However, the use of BWCs also raises concerns about privacy. Policies must be in place to regulate data storage, access, and retention, ensuring that the privacy rights of individuals are protected. For example, clear guidelines are needed regarding when cameras should be activated and deactivated, as well as protocols for redacting sensitive information from recordings before they are released to the public.
Another significant advancement is the use of data analytics and predictive policing. These tools analyze crime data to identify patterns and predict future crime hotspots. By allocating resources to these areas, law enforcement can proactively deter crime and improve public safety. For example, some police departments are using algorithms to analyze past crime data, demographic information, and even social media activity to identify individuals at risk of committing or becoming victims of crime. This allows officers to intervene with targeted prevention efforts, such as providing social services or offering support to at-risk individuals. While these tools hold great promise, they also raise concerns about bias and

discrimination. If the data used to train these algorithms reflects existing biases in the criminal justice system, the algorithms may perpetuate these biases, leading to disproportionate targeting of certain communities. For example, if police have historically focused on drug enforcement in low-income neighborhoods, the data may suggest that crime is more prevalent in those areas, leading to increased police presence even if the actual crime rate is not higher. To mitigate these risks, it is essential to ensure that algorithms are transparent, regularly audited for bias, and used in conjunction with human oversight.

The integration of geographic information systems (GIS) into policing strategies has also proven invaluable. GIS technology allows law enforcement to map crime incidents, analyze spatial patterns, and identify areas with high crime concentrations. This information can be used to optimize patrol routes, deploy resources more effectively, and develop targeted crime prevention strategies. For instance, GIS can be used to identify areas with high rates of burglaries, allowing police to increase patrols in those areas, distribute crime prevention tips to residents, and work with local businesses to improve security measures. Furthermore, GIS can be used to track the movement of offenders, monitor parolees, and investigate complex criminal networks. However, the effectiveness of GIS depends on the quality and accuracy of the data used. If crime data is incomplete or inaccurate, the resulting maps and analyses may be misleading, leading to ineffective resource allocation and misguided strategies. Therefore, it is essential to invest in robust data collection and management systems to ensure that GIS is used effectively.

Advancements in forensic science have also significantly enhanced law enforcement capabilities. DNA analysis, for example, has become an indispensable tool for identifying suspects, exonerating the wrongly accused, and solving cold cases. The development of rapid DNA testing technologies has further expedited the process, allowing law enforcement to obtain results in a matter of hours rather than weeks. This can be particularly useful in time-sensitive investigations, such as sexual assault cases. However, the use of DNA evidence also raises concerns about privacy and potential for misuse. DNA databases, which contain genetic information from millions of individuals, are vulnerable to hacking and unauthorized access. Furthermore, there are concerns about the potential for discriminatory use of DNA data, such as targeting individuals based on their genetic predisposition to certain diseases or behaviors. To address these concerns, it is essential to implement strict security measures to protect DNA databases and establish clear ethical guidelines for the collection, storage, and use of DNA evidence.

Finally, communication and information sharing have been revolutionized by technology. Modern police departments rely on sophisticated communication networks, including mobile devices, secure radio systems, and online platforms, to coordinate operations and share information in real-time. This allows officers to respond more quickly and effectively to emergencies, track suspects, and collaborate with other agencies. For example, many police departments use mobile data terminals (MDTs) in their patrol cars, allowing officers to access criminal records, dispatch information, and other critical data from the field. These tools can significantly improve officer safety and efficiency. However, reliance on technology also creates vulnerabilities. Communication networks can be disrupted by cyberattacks or natural disasters, potentially hindering law enforcement's ability to respond to emergencies. To mitigate these risks, it is essential to develop robust cybersecurity protocols and contingency plans to ensure that communication systems remain operational in the event of a disruption. It's also key to foster a culture of continuous learning and adaptation within law enforcement agencies, ensuring that officers are equipped with the knowledge and skills needed to use these technologies effectively and ethically. By embracing technological advancements while addressing the associated challenges, policing can become more effective, efficient, and accountable, ultimately contributing to a safer and more just society.

4 Chapter 4: Judicial System Enhancements

Judicial systems, the cornerstone of any civilized society, often face immense pressure to adapt and evolve to meet the ever-changing landscape of criminal behavior and societal expectations. Ensuring a fair and impartial judicial process isn't just a legal imperative; it's a fundamental pillar of public trust and social order. It's about more than just the strict application of laws; it's about creating a system that is perceived as equitable, unbiased, and truly committed to justice for all individuals, regardless of their background or circumstances. Enhancing the judicial system therefore calls for a multi-faceted approach, addressing both the structural components and the inherent human elements that can influence outcomes.

Achieving fair and impartial justice begins with addressing potential sources of bias at every stage of the judicial process. This includes rigorous selection and training for judges, ensuring a diverse pool of candidates who reflect the communities they serve. Robust ethical guidelines and accountability mechanisms are also crucial to prevent conflicts of interest and maintain judicial integrity. Jury selection processes must be meticulously designed to avoid discriminatory practices, ensuring that juries represent a cross-section of society and are capable of rendering impartial verdicts. In addition to these safeguards, access to legal representation is paramount. Individuals facing criminal charges must have access to competent legal counsel, regardless of their financial means. Public defender systems should be adequately funded and staffed to provide effective representation to those who cannot afford private attorneys. This ensures a level playing field and prevents disparities in outcomes based solely on economic status. We also need to provide linguistic accessibility, meaning interpreting, and documentation.

Sentencing guidelines play a pivotal role in shaping the outcomes of criminal cases, and their structure and application can have a significant impact on fairness and proportionality. While guidelines aim to reduce disparities and ensure consistency, they can sometimes lead to unintended consequences, such as excessively harsh penalties for certain offenses. Reform efforts should focus on refining sentencing guidelines to better reflect the nuances of individual cases and prioritize rehabilitation over retribution. This may involve incorporating factors such as the offender's background, the circumstances of the crime, and the potential for rehabilitation into the sentencing calculus. Alternative sentencing options, such as drug treatment programs, community service, and restorative justice initiatives, should be explored and expanded to address the underlying causes of crime and promote offender accountability. These alternatives can be particularly effective for non-violent offenses, offering a more constructive approach to punishment that reduces recidivism and promotes reintegration into society. Restorative justice, in particular, provides an opportunity for victims and offenders to engage in dialogue, allowing victims to express their harm and offenders to take responsibility for their actions. This process can lead to healing for victims, accountability for offenders, and a greater sense of justice for the community.

Technological advancements offer unprecedented opportunities to enhance the efficiency and transparency of the judicial system. Electronic case management systems can streamline administrative processes, reduce paperwork, and improve access to information for all stakeholders. Video conferencing can facilitate remote court appearances, reducing travel time and costs for witnesses, defendants, and attorneys. Data analytics can be used to identify patterns of bias in sentencing and decision-making, allowing for targeted interventions to promote fairness and equity. However, the use of technology in the judicial system must be carefully implemented to avoid unintended consequences. Privacy concerns must be addressed through robust data security measures and clear guidelines on the collection, storage, and use of personal information. Algorithmic bias must be actively mitigated to ensure that technology does not perpetuate or exacerbate existing inequalities. Access to technology must also be equitable, ensuring that all individuals, regardless of their socioeconomic status or location, have the means to participate in the judicial process. It has been shown that implementing Artificial Intelligence in the courtroom can be dangerous and extremely biased in a way we might not even think about.

Continuous evaluation and reform are essential to ensure that the judicial system remains responsive to the needs of society and committed to the principles of fairness, impartiality, and justice. Regular audits of court processes, sentencing practices, and legal representation systems should be conducted to identify areas for improvement. Feedback from victims, offenders, attorneys, and community members should be actively solicited and incorporated into reform efforts. Collaboration between policymakers, legal professionals, academics, and community organizations is crucial to develop and implement evidence-based reforms that address the root causes of crime and promote a more just and equitable society. The judicial system is not a static entity; it must constantly adapt and evolve to meet the challenges of a changing world. By embracing innovation, promoting transparency, and prioritizing fairness, we can create a judicial system that truly serves the interests of justice and contributes to the well-being of all members of society.

Finally, improving communication and transparency within the judicial system is vital for building public trust and ensuring accountability. Plain language summaries of court procedures, legal rights, and sentencing options should be readily available to the public. Court proceedings should be open to the public, except in limited circumstances where confidentiality is necessary to protect victims or witnesses. Data on court caseloads, demographics of defendants, and sentencing outcomes should be publicly accessible, allowing for scrutiny and analysis. In addition to providing information to the public, the judicial system must also be responsive to community concerns. Regular town hall meetings and community forums should be held to provide opportunities for dialogue between court officials, law enforcement, and residents. These forums can serve as a platform for addressing concerns, gathering feedback, and building relationships of trust. Ultimately, a fair, impartial, and effective judicial system is not just a legal imperative; it is a moral one. It is a reflection of our commitment to the principles of justice, equality, and human dignity. By investing in enhancements to the judicial system, we invest in a more just and equitable society for all.

4.1 Fair and Impartial Justice

Fair and Impartial Justice

The cornerstone of any legitimate system designed to address criminal conduct lies in its ability to deliver justice that is both fair and impartial. This is not merely a lofty ideal, but a pragmatic necessity. If individuals perceive the system as biased or unjust, they are less likely to respect its authority, cooperate with its processes, or accept its outcomes, ultimately undermining the goal of societal calm and stability. Fairness dictates that every person, regardless of their background, social status, or alleged offense, receives equal treatment under the law. This means ensuring access to competent legal representation, a transparent judicial process, and a decision based solely on the evidence presented, free from prejudice or undue influence.

Achieving this ideal requires constant vigilance and proactive measures to address potential sources of bias within the system. One critical area is addressing systemic inequalities. Racial and socioeconomic disparities often permeate the criminal justice system, leading to disproportionate rates of arrest, conviction, and incarceration for certain groups. These disparities can stem from a variety of factors, including implicit bias in policing practices, unequal access to quality education and employment opportunities, and the lingering effects of historical discrimination. Combating these inequalities requires a multi-pronged approach. Law enforcement agencies must implement training programs to address implicit bias and promote fair and equitable policing practices. Prosecutors need to carefully review cases to ensure that charging decisions are not influenced by race or socioeconomic status. Courts must be vigilant in protecting the rights of all defendants and ensuring that they receive a fair trial. Furthermore, investment in underserved communities can help to address the root causes of crime and reduce the likelihood of individuals becoming involved in the criminal justice system in the first place.

Another crucial aspect of fair and impartial justice is ensuring the competence and integrity of legal professionals. Lawyers, judges, and prosecutors all play vital roles in upholding the principles of justice, and their conduct must be beyond reproach. Adequate training and resources are essential to ensure that legal professionals are equipped to handle complex cases effectively and ethically. Regular evaluations and oversight mechanisms can help to identify and address instances of misconduct or incompetence. In addition, measures should be taken to promote diversity within the legal profession, ensuring that individuals from all backgrounds have the opportunity to serve in these important roles. A diverse judiciary and legal community can bring a broader range of perspectives and experiences to the justice system, enhancing its fairness and legitimacy. Moreover, transparency is paramount. Court proceedings should be open to the public, and records should be readily accessible. This allows for scrutiny and accountability, helping to ensure that the system operates fairly and impartially.

Sentencing practices also play a critical role in achieving fair and impartial justice. Disparities in sentencing can undermine public confidence in the system and perpetuate inequalities. While sentencing guidelines can help to promote consistency, they must be carefully designed to avoid unintended consequences. Rigid guidelines can sometimes lead to unjust outcomes in individual cases, failing to account for mitigating circumstances or the unique characteristics of the offender. A more nuanced approach to sentencing is needed, one that considers both the severity of the offense and the individual circumstances of the offender. Alternatives to incarceration, such as probation, community service, and restorative justice programs, should be explored as options for non-violent offenders, particularly those with mental health issues or substance abuse problems. These alternatives can be more effective at promoting rehabilitation and reducing recidivism than simply locking people up. Furthermore, victims of crime must be given a voice in the sentencing process. They should have the opportunity to express their views and provide input to the court. This can help to ensure that the sentencing outcome is just and takes into account the harm that has been caused.

Beyond the formal legal processes, public perception of fairness and impartiality is crucial. If people do not believe that the system is fair, they are less likely to cooperate with law enforcement, report crimes, or participate in the judicial process. Building trust in the justice system requires a commitment to transparency, accountability, and community engagement. Law enforcement agencies should strive to build positive relationships with the communities they serve, fostering open communication and mutual respect. Community policing initiatives can be particularly effective in this regard. Prosecutors and judges should also engage with the community, explaining their decisions and addressing concerns. Public education programs can help to promote a better understanding of the justice system and its role in maintaining societal calm and stability.

Finally, it's important to acknowledge that achieving fair and impartial justice is an ongoing process, not a destination. The system must constantly adapt and evolve to address new challenges and ensure that it remains true to its fundamental principles. This requires a willingness to learn from past mistakes, to listen to diverse perspectives, and to embrace innovation. Only through continuous improvement can we hope to create a truly just and equitable system for all.

In my experience, creating a judicial system perceived as fair also requires acknowledging and addressing historical injustices. These past wrongs can cast a long shadow, creating distrust and resentment that undermine the legitimacy of the present-day system. Restorative justice practices, where offenders take responsibility for their actions and work to repair the harm they have caused, can be a powerful tool for healing and reconciliation. These practices can involve dialogue between victims and offenders, community service projects, or other forms of restitution. By actively addressing past wrongs and seeking to make amends, the justice system can begin to rebuild trust and foster a sense of fairness and equity. I believe in the power of a system where everyone feels safe, respected, and confident that justice will prevail, irrespective of their background. This is not just a matter of enforcing laws; it's about creating a society where justice truly serves all its members.

4.2 Sentencing Guidelines and Reform

Sentencing is arguably the most critical decision a judge makes. It represents the culmination of the judicial process, balancing the need for punishment, deterrence, rehabilitation, and victim restoration. The ideal sentencing framework aims to achieve these objectives fairly and consistently, but the reality is often far more complex. This chapter will explore the nuances of sentencing guidelines and potential reforms to enhance the judicial system.

Sentencing guidelines emerged as a response to widespread disparities in sentencing practices. Before their implementation, judges wielded considerable discretion, leading to situations where similar offenses could result in drastically different outcomes depending on the judge, jurisdiction, or even the defendant's background. These disparities undermined public confidence in the fairness of the justice system. Guidelines aim to reduce this inconsistency by providing a structured framework for determining appropriate sentences. Typically, they involve a matrix that considers factors such as the severity of the crime, the offender's criminal history, and any mitigating or aggravating circumstances. By assigning numerical values to these factors, the guidelines generate a recommended sentencing range. While judges retain some discretion to deviate from these guidelines, they must provide a written justification for doing so. Despite the intention of minimizing disparities, sentencing guidelines haven't fully eradicated them. Critics argue that they can lead to overly rigid and formulaic sentencing, failing to account for the unique circumstances of each case. Moreover, research suggests that implicit biases can still influence how judges apply the guidelines, resulting in disparities based on race, ethnicity, or socioeconomic status.

One promising avenue for reform lies in incorporating risk assessment tools into the sentencing process. These tools use statistical models to predict an offender's likelihood of re-offending based on a range of factors, such as age, education, employment history, and substance abuse patterns. By identifying offenders who pose a low risk of re-offending, judges can consider alternative sentencing options, such as probation, community service, or restorative justice programs. This approach not only reduces incarceration rates but also allows resources to be directed towards higher-risk offenders who require more intensive supervision and intervention. However, the use of risk assessment tools is not without controversy. Concerns have been raised about their accuracy and potential for bias. If the tools are based on data that reflects existing disparities in the criminal justice system, they may perpetuate and exacerbate those disparities. For example, if individuals from certain racial or ethnic groups are disproportionately arrested and convicted for certain crimes, the risk assessment tool may unfairly label individuals from those groups as high-risk. To mitigate these risks, it's crucial to ensure that risk assessment tools are rigorously validated for accuracy and fairness across different demographic groups. Furthermore, the tools should be used as one factor among many in the sentencing decision, not as the sole determinant.

Restorative justice offers a fundamentally different approach to sentencing, one that focuses on repairing the harm caused by the crime and promoting reconciliation between the offender, the victim, and the community. Instead of solely focusing on punishment, restorative justice processes involve bringing together all parties affected by the crime to discuss its impact and determine how the offender can make amends. This may involve restitution, community service, or even a formal apology. Restorative justice has been shown to be particularly effective in cases involving juvenile offenders and non-violent crimes. Studies have found that it can reduce recidivism rates, increase victim satisfaction, and promote a greater sense of accountability among offenders. However, restorative justice is not appropriate for all cases. It requires the voluntary participation of both the offender and the victim, and it may not be suitable for cases involving serious violence or where the offender denies responsibility for the crime.

Another important aspect of sentencing reform is addressing the underlying causes of crime. As highlighted in earlier chapters, factors such as poverty, lack of education, and substance abuse can contribute to criminal behavior. By investing in programs that address these root causes, we can reduce the likelihood of individuals becoming involved in the criminal justice system in the first place. This may involve expanding access to education and job training, providing affordable housing, and offering treatment for substance abuse and mental health disorders. Furthermore, it's crucial to implement policies that promote racial and economic equality, ensuring that all individuals have the opportunity to succeed. These policies not only reduce crime but also create a more just and equitable society.

Finally, effective sentencing reform requires ongoing monitoring and evaluation. It's essential to track the impact of different sentencing practices on recidivism rates, incarceration rates, and racial disparities. This data can then be used to refine sentencing guidelines and identify areas where further reforms are needed. Furthermore, it's important to involve stakeholders from all parts of the criminal justice system in the reform process, including judges, prosecutors, defense attorneys, probation officers, and community members. By working together, we can create a sentencing system that is fair, effective, and promotes public safety. The path to better sentencing lies in embracing evidence-based practices, addressing systemic inequalities, and fostering a culture of accountability and rehabilitation.

5 Chapter 5: Rehabilitation and Reintegration

Rehabilitation and reintegration represent the cornerstone of a long-term strategy aimed at mitigating the effects of criminal conduct and fostering lasting societal calm. It moves beyond the immediate response of punishment and addresses the underlying factors that contribute to recidivism. Meaningful reform and successful reintegration are not merely acts of compassion, but rather, strategically vital components of a comprehensive system designed to reduce crime rates and improve community well-being. This chapter argues for a radical shift in perspective, viewing those who have offended not as permanently defined by their past actions, but as individuals capable of growth, change, and positive contributions to society. This approach necessitates a holistic strategy that tackles the systemic issues within correctional facilities, provides opportunities for skills development, and offers unwavering support to those transitioning back into civilian life.

Correctional facility reform is paramount to the success of any rehabilitation program. Often, these institutions are plagued by overcrowding, violence, and a lack of resources, creating environments that reinforce negative behaviors rather than fostering positive change. The focus must shift from solely punitive measures to creating therapeutic environments where inmates can address the root causes of their criminal behavior. This includes providing access to mental health services, substance abuse treatment programs, and educational opportunities. Investing in well-trained and compassionate correctional staff is also crucial. These individuals should be equipped with the skills necessary to de-escalate conflicts, provide guidance, and act as positive role models. Furthermore, incorporating restorative justice practices within correctional facilities can help inmates take responsibility for their actions and begin the process of reconciliation with victims and the community. This might involve victim-offender mediation programs or community impact panels where inmates can hear directly from those affected by their crimes. By transforming correctional facilities into environments that prioritize rehabilitation, we can significantly increase the likelihood of successful reintegration.

Beyond addressing the internal environment of correctional facilities, investment in vocational training programs is a necessary step. One of the most significant barriers to successful reintegration is the lack of employment opportunities. Many ex-offenders struggle to find jobs due to their criminal records, lack of education, and absence of marketable skills. Vocational training programs can equip them with the skills needed to compete in the job market, increasing their chances of finding stable employment and becoming self-sufficient. These programs should be tailored to the needs of the local economy, offering training in high-demand industries such as construction, manufacturing, technology, and healthcare. Partnerships with local businesses can provide valuable opportunities for apprenticeships and job placement after release. In addition to technical skills, these programs should also focus on developing soft skills such as communication, teamwork, and problem-solving, which are essential for success in any workplace. By providing ex-offenders with the tools they need to secure employment, we can reduce their reliance on criminal activity and increase their chances of becoming productive members of society.

However, even with adequate training and skills, ex-offenders often face significant challenges in navigating the complex process of reintegration. This is where comprehensive support systems become essential. These systems should address a range of needs, including housing, healthcare, job placement, and counseling. Many ex-offenders struggle to find stable housing due to discriminatory practices and a lack of affordable options. Providing access to transitional housing programs can offer a safe and supportive environment as they search for permanent housing. Similarly, access to healthcare is crucial, particularly for those with mental health or substance abuse issues. These individuals may require ongoing treatment and support to maintain their recovery and avoid relapse. Job placement services can help ex-offenders connect with employers who are willing to give them a second chance, providing resume writing assistance, interview coaching, and job search support. Counseling services can address the emotional and psychological challenges associated with reintegration, helping ex-offenders cope with stigma, build healthy relationships, and develop coping mechanisms for dealing with stress and temptation.

Moreover, fostering a sense of community support is crucial for successful reintegration. This involves educating the public about the challenges faced by ex-offenders and encouraging them to offer support and understanding. Community-based organizations can play a vital role in providing mentorship, support groups, and other resources to help ex-offenders connect with positive role models and build social connections. Churches, synagogues, and other faith-based organizations can also provide spiritual guidance and support. By creating a welcoming and supportive community, we can help ex-offenders feel less isolated and more motivated to stay on the right track.

Finally, it's important to acknowledge that rehabilitation and reintegration are not one-size-fits-all solutions. Different individuals have different needs and require tailored approaches. Some may benefit from intensive therapy, while others may thrive in vocational training programs. Regular monitoring and evaluation are essential to ensure that programs are effective and meeting the needs of the participants. Flexibility and adaptability are key to success. It is necessary to be willing to adjust strategies and approaches as needed to maximize the impact. By investing in rehabilitation and reintegration programs, we can reduce recidivism, improve community safety, and create a more just and equitable society for all. It's not merely a matter of offering a second chance, but strategically building a safer society through proactive and holistic approaches. The positive effect will permeate from individuals, families, and communities.

5.1 Correctional Facility Reform

Correctional facilities, often seen as the end point of the criminal justice system, are in reality, a critical juncture where genuine reform can either take root or be irrevocably stifled. The old model of simply warehousing inmates is demonstrably ineffective, costly, and contributes to the cycle of recidivism. We need a new vision, one that prioritizes rehabilitation, skill development, and the successful reintegration of offenders back into society. The goal isn't just punishment; it's to reduce future crime.

Consider the current landscape: overcrowded prisons, understaffed and undertrained correctional officers, and a dearth of meaningful programs designed to address the underlying causes of criminal behavior. This toxic combination creates an environment ripe for violence, despair, and ultimately, a return to crime upon release. It's a broken system, and it's costing us all dearly, not just financially, but in terms of societal safety and lost potential. We have to move beyond the punitive mindset and embrace a more restorative approach.

The cornerstone of correctional facility reform lies in prioritizing individualized rehabilitation plans. This means moving away from a one-size-fits-all approach and investing in comprehensive assessments to understand each inmate's specific needs, risk factors, and potential for positive change. What are their educational deficits? What are their mental health concerns? What skills do they need to secure legitimate employment? Answering these questions is paramount.

Furthermore, robust vocational training programs are essential. Too often, inmates are released with no marketable skills, making it incredibly difficult to find employment and reintegrate into society. We need to provide them with opportunities to learn trades, develop technical skills, and gain valuable work experience while incarcerated. This not only increases their chances of securing employment upon release but also instills a sense of purpose and self-worth. Partnering with local businesses and industries to create apprenticeship programs within correctional facilities can provide invaluable real-world experience and increase the likelihood of job placement after release.

Mental health services must also be readily available and integrated into the rehabilitation process. Many inmates suffer from mental health issues, often exacerbated by the trauma of incarceration. Providing access to therapy, counseling, and medication is crucial for addressing these underlying issues and preventing future criminal behavior. It is paramount to acknowledge that many criminal behaviors are directly related to underlying mental health conditions, and addressing those is key to long term success. Ignoring these needs is not only inhumane, but also a public safety risk.

Another critical aspect of correctional facility reform is improving the conditions of confinement. Overcrowding, poor sanitation, and a lack of access to basic necessities can contribute to violence, unrest, and a sense of hopelessness. We need to ensure that inmates are treated with dignity and respect, and that their basic needs are met. This includes providing adequate healthcare, nutritious meals, and opportunities for recreation and exercise. A humane environment is a crucial foundation for rehabilitation.

Equally important is the training and development of correctional officers. They are on the front lines, interacting with inmates daily and playing a critical role in fostering a safe and rehabilitative environment. Providing them with adequate training in de-escalation techniques, conflict resolution, and mental health awareness is essential. Furthermore, we need to create a culture of support and mentorship within correctional facilities, where officers feel valued and empowered to make a positive impact on the lives of inmates. Investing in our correctional officers is an investment in the safety and well-being of our communities.

Successful reintegration into society requires a comprehensive support system that extends beyond the prison walls. This includes providing access to housing assistance, job placement services, and ongoing counseling and support. Many ex-offenders struggle to find housing or employment due to their criminal records, making it difficult to rebuild their lives. We need to remove these barriers and provide them with the resources they need to succeed. Mentorship programs, connecting ex-offenders with positive role models and support networks, can also be incredibly valuable in helping them stay on the right track.

Technological integration also has the potential to drive correctional facility reform, the implementation of advanced security systems, data analytics, and educational platforms can improve operational efficiency, enhance safety, and support rehabilitation efforts. For example, body cameras for correctional officers can increase transparency and accountability, while data analytics can identify patterns of behavior and inform targeted interventions. Investing in technology can make our correctional facilities safer, more efficient, and more effective at rehabilitating offenders.

Finally, true correctional facility reform requires a shift in societal attitudes towards crime and punishment. We need to move beyond the simplistic notion of "an eye for an eye" and embrace a more nuanced understanding of the complexities of criminal behavior. This requires open and honest conversations about the root causes of crime, the effectiveness of different approaches to rehabilitation, and the importance of providing opportunities for second chances. By changing the way we think about crime, we can create a more just and compassionate society that is truly committed to reducing recidivism and building safer communities for all.

Implementing these reforms will not be easy. It will require significant investment, political will, and a willingness to challenge the status quo. But the potential benefits are enormous: reduced crime rates, safer communities, and a more just and equitable society for all. It's time to move beyond the outdated model of punishment and embrace a new vision of correctional facilities as centers of rehabilitation and transformation. The future of our communities depends on it.

5.2 Vocational Training Programs

Vocational Training Programs represent a cornerstone in the rehabilitation process, offering individuals entangled in the criminal justice system a pathway towards sustainable employment and a crime-free life. These programs are not merely about teaching a skill; they are about instilling a sense of purpose, self-worth, and responsibility, effectively disrupting the cycle of recidivism. My own experience working with ex-offenders has shown me firsthand the transformative power of acquiring a trade, providing them with not only a means of financial independence but also a renewed sense of belonging and contribution to society.

The landscape of vocational training is incredibly diverse, encompassing a wide array of skills tailored to meet the demands of the local job market. Construction trades, such as carpentry, plumbing, and electrical work, consistently offer high demand and relatively good wages. Culinary arts programs provide opportunities in restaurants, catering services, and even entrepreneurship. Automotive repair, welding, and other manufacturing skills are always valuable, particularly in areas with industrial sectors. Technology-focused training, including coding, computer repair, and data entry, is becoming increasingly relevant in our digital age. The key is to carefully assess the needs of the local economy and align training programs accordingly, ensuring that graduates possess skills that are actually in demand and can readily translate into employment. Furthermore, it's beneficial to offer a range of programs, catering to different interests, aptitudes, and educational levels.

Effective vocational training programs extend far beyond simply teaching technical skills. They integrate essential life skills training, including resume writing, interview preparation, financial literacy, and conflict resolution. Many individuals entering these programs lack basic workplace etiquette and communication skills, which can be significant barriers to employment. Addressing these gaps is crucial for ensuring their long-term success. Mentorship programs, pairing trainees with experienced professionals in their chosen field, can provide invaluable guidance, support, and networking opportunities. These mentors can offer insights into the industry, help navigate workplace challenges, and serve as positive role models. Additionally, programs should incorporate elements of cognitive behavioral therapy (CBT) to address underlying behavioral patterns and thought processes that may have contributed to their involvement in crime. CBT can help individuals develop healthier coping mechanisms, manage anger and impulsivity, and make more responsible choices.

Successful implementation of vocational training programs necessitates strong partnerships between correctional facilities, community colleges, technical schools, and local employers. Correctional facilities play a critical role in identifying and preparing inmates for participation in these programs. They can provide basic education, pre-vocational training, and assessments to determine individual aptitudes and interests. Community colleges and technical schools offer the expertise and resources needed to deliver high-quality vocational training, often providing certified instructors, state-of-the-art equipment, and industry-recognized credentials. Local employers are essential partners in providing internships, apprenticeships, and ultimately, job opportunities for graduates. These partnerships must be carefully cultivated and maintained, ensuring clear communication, shared goals, and mutual accountability. Furthermore, government funding and private philanthropy play a vital role in supporting these programs, providing resources for training materials, equipment, instructor salaries, and support services.

Evaluating the effectiveness of vocational training programs is crucial for continuous improvement and ensuring accountability. Recidivism rates, employment rates, and wage levels are key indicators of success. Tracking these metrics over time provides valuable insights into the impact of the programs and identifies areas for improvement. Surveys and interviews with graduates, employers, and program staff can provide qualitative data, offering a deeper understanding of the challenges and successes of the programs. This data should be used to inform program design, curriculum development, and service delivery, ensuring that the programs are meeting the needs of both participants and the community. Independent evaluations, conducted by external organizations, can provide an objective assessment of program effectiveness and identify best practices.

However, even the most well-designed and implemented vocational training programs face significant challenges. Stigma associated with a criminal record remains a major barrier to employment, despite federal and state laws aimed at reducing discrimination. Many employers are hesitant to hire individuals with a history of incarceration, fearing potential risks to their business or reputation. Addressing this stigma requires concerted efforts to educate employers about the benefits of hiring ex-offenders, highlighting their skills, motivation, and potential contributions to the workforce. Offering tax incentives or other financial benefits to employers who hire ex-offenders can further encourage their participation. Adequate funding for vocational training programs is often lacking, particularly in states with tight budgets. Competition for resources is fierce, and vocational training programs often struggle to secure the funding needed to operate effectively. Advocating for increased funding and demonstrating the cost-effectiveness of these programs are essential for ensuring their sustainability.

Moving forward, the future of vocational training programs lies in innovation and adaptation. Embracing technology and incorporating online learning platforms can expand access to training opportunities, particularly for individuals in rural or underserved areas. Developing specialized training programs tailored to emerging industries, such as renewable energy and healthcare, can equip participants with skills that are in high demand. Integrating entrepreneurial training into vocational programs can empower individuals to start their own businesses, creating new jobs and contributing to economic growth. Ultimately, vocational training programs are a critical investment in our communities, providing a pathway to redemption and a second chance for individuals who have made mistakes. By equipping them with the skills, knowledge, and support they need to succeed, we can reduce recidivism, improve public safety, and build a more just and equitable society. The success of these programs is not just measured in reduced crime rates; it's measured in the transformed lives of individuals who find purpose, dignity, and hope through meaningful employment. And that, in my view, is a truly invaluable contribution to societal calm and stability.

Let's consider the case of "Project New Start" in a hypothetical mid-sized city struggling with a rise in property crime linked to repeat offenders. This program would partner with the local community college to offer certification programs in high-demand trades like HVAC repair, plumbing, and electrical work. Inmates nearing their release would be carefully vetted and offered the opportunity to participate. The program wouldn't just focus on technical skills. It would also include intensive workshops on financial literacy, conflict resolution, and job readiness. Local businesses would be actively involved, offering internships and guaranteeing interviews to graduates. A dedicated case manager would work with each participant to address individual needs, providing support with housing, transportation, and mental health services. Furthermore, the program would actively work to combat employer stigma through public awareness campaigns and by offering liability insurance to businesses that hire graduates. Rigorous evaluation would track recidivism rates, employment rates, and wage levels, allowing for continuous improvement and ensuring the program's long-term effectiveness.

5.3 Support Systems for Ex-Offenders

The transition from incarceration back into society represents a pivotal moment for ex-offenders, and their successful reintegration hinges significantly on the strength and availability of robust support systems. These systems act as a crucial safety net, mitigating the challenges of finding employment, securing housing, and navigating the complexities of rebuilding a life after serving time. Without adequate support, the risk of recidivism dramatically increases, perpetuating a cycle of crime and incarceration. It's about more than just reducing crime rates; it's about fostering a more just and equitable society where individuals are given a second chance to become productive members of their communities.

A cornerstone of any effective support system for ex-offenders is employment assistance. Many formerly incarcerated individuals face significant barriers to finding work, including employer reluctance, lack of job skills, and the stigma associated with a criminal record. Vocational training programs, as mentioned earlier, play a vital role in equipping ex-offenders with marketable skills, but these programs alone are not enough. Job placement services are essential to connect individuals with employers who are willing to give them a chance. These services can provide resume writing assistance, interview coaching, and help navigating the application process. Furthermore, advocating for policies that encourage employers to hire ex-offenders, such as tax incentives or "ban the box" initiatives, can significantly improve their employment prospects. Ultimately, securing stable employment provides ex-offenders with financial independence, a sense of purpose, and a pathway to self-sufficiency, reducing the likelihood of re-offending. Overcoming these hurdles unlocks their potential, turning them into taxpayers and contributors to the economy.

Beyond employment, stable housing is another critical need for ex-offenders. Many face homelessness or housing instability upon release, making it difficult to maintain employment, attend counseling, or meet parole requirements. Supportive housing programs provide temporary or long-term housing, often coupled with supportive services such as case management, substance abuse counseling, and life skills training. These programs create a stable and supportive environment where ex-offenders can focus on their rehabilitation and reintegration. Additionally, advocating for policies that address housing discrimination against individuals with criminal records is crucial. Landlords often deny housing to ex-offenders, perpetuating a cycle of homelessness and instability. Fair housing laws and community-based initiatives can help break down these barriers and ensure that ex-offenders have access to safe and affordable housing. The presence of a reliable roof over one's head is fundamental for stability and a necessary building block for a successful return to society.

Mental health and substance abuse treatment are also essential components of a comprehensive support system. Many ex-offenders have experienced trauma, mental health issues, or substance abuse problems that contributed to their involvement in the criminal justice system. Providing access to counseling, therapy, and support groups can help them address these underlying issues and develop coping mechanisms for managing stress, anxiety, and depression. Substance abuse treatment programs, including detoxification, rehabilitation, and aftercare services, are crucial for preventing relapse and promoting long-term recovery. These programs should be evidence-based and tailored to the individual needs of each ex-offender. By addressing mental health and substance abuse issues, support systems can help ex-offenders break free from the cycle of addiction and develop healthier, more productive lives. Ignoring these critical needs almost guarantees a return to previous harmful behaviors. Reintegration also necessitates strong social support networks. Isolation and lack of social connection can be significant risk factors for recidivism. Support systems should facilitate connections with family, friends, and community members who can provide emotional support, encouragement, and guidance. Mentoring programs, where ex-offenders are paired with positive role models, can be particularly effective. Mentors can provide practical assistance, such as helping with job searches or navigating the legal system, as well as emotional support and encouragement. Community-based organizations, such as faith-based groups or neighborhood associations, can also play a vital role in providing social support and fostering a sense of belonging. Building these networks creates a safety net of positive relationships that can help ex-offenders stay on track and avoid re-offending. It's about creating a sense of belonging and showing them that they are not alone in their journey.

Finally, effective support systems must be coordinated and collaborative. Many different agencies and organizations are involved in providing services to ex-offenders, including correctional facilities, probation departments, social service agencies, and community-based organizations. These entities must work together seamlessly to ensure that ex-offenders receive the comprehensive and coordinated support they need. Case management services play a crucial role in coordinating these services, helping ex-offenders navigate the complex system and access the resources they need. Technology can also be used to improve coordination and communication among service providers. Shared databases and electronic case management systems can help track progress, identify gaps in services, and ensure that ex-offenders receive timely and appropriate support. A fragmented approach will only lead to frustration and failure. A unified front is essential for maximizing the impact of support services and promoting successful reintegration.

6 Chapter 6: Addressing Specific Crime Types

Let's dive into the details of tackling different crime types. No single strategy works for every criminal activity; a nuanced approach is essential. We must tailor our efforts to the specific characteristics of each crime, understanding its motivations, patterns, and impact on the community. This chapter focuses on three broad categories: violent crime, property crime, and cybercrime, each requiring its own set of preventative and responsive measures. It's not just about reacting after a crime occurs, it's about proactively dismantling the conditions that allow these crimes to flourish.

Violent crime, encompassing offenses like homicide, assault, robbery, and sexual assault, demands immediate and decisive action. These crimes inflict profound trauma on victims, erode community trust, and create a climate of fear. Combating violent crime requires a multi-pronged strategy, starting with targeted policing in high-crime areas. This doesn't mean indiscriminate sweeps; it means deploying resources strategically based on data-driven analysis of crime hotspots and patterns. Focused deterrence strategies, where law enforcement partners with community stakeholders to directly address individuals at high risk of committing violence, have proven effective. These strategies involve clearly communicating the consequences of violence, offering opportunities for positive change, and consistently enforcing the law. It involves a community, law enforcement, and social services working together. Gun violence, a significant contributor to violent crime rates, requires specific attention. This includes efforts to reduce the availability of illegal firearms, strengthen background checks, and address straw purchasing. Equally important is investing in community-based violence intervention programs. These programs employ credible messengers – individuals with lived experience – to mediate conflicts, de-escalate tensions, and provide support to victims and perpetrators of violence. Moreover, addressing the underlying causes of violent crime is crucial. Factors such as poverty, lack of opportunity, and social inequality can contribute to a cycle of violence. Investing in education, job training, and affordable housing can help break this cycle and create safer communities.

Property crime, including burglary, larceny, motor vehicle theft, and arson, while often perceived as less serious than violent crime, can have a significant impact on individuals and communities. It erodes residents' sense of security, disrupts businesses, and drains economic resources. Controlling property crime requires a combination of prevention and enforcement strategies. Target hardening measures, such as installing security systems, improving lighting, and reinforcing doors and windows, can deter burglars and reduce the likelihood of successful break-ins. Community watch programs, where residents work together to monitor their neighborhoods and report suspicious activity, can also be effective in preventing property crime. These programs foster a sense of collective responsibility and create a visible deterrent to criminals. Furthermore, addressing the underlying causes of property crime, such as drug addiction and economic hardship, is essential. Providing access to treatment programs, job training, and financial assistance can help reduce the motivation for individuals to engage in property crime. Law enforcement plays a critical role in investigating property crimes, apprehending offenders, and recovering stolen property. Using data analytics to identify crime trends and patterns, police can deploy resources strategically and target repeat offenders. Collaboration between law enforcement and businesses is also important. Businesses can implement security measures, such as installing surveillance cameras and training employees to recognize and report suspicious activity, to deter shoplifting and other forms of property crime.

Cybercrime, an increasingly prevalent threat in our interconnected world, encompasses a wide range of offenses, including hacking, phishing, identity theft, and online fraud. Cybercrime can target individuals, businesses, and even governments, causing significant financial losses, reputational damage, and disruption of services. Preventing and responding to cybercrime requires a multi-layered approach. Education and awareness are paramount. Individuals and businesses need to be educated about the risks of cybercrime and how to protect themselves. This includes teaching people how to recognize phishing scams, create strong passwords, and protect their personal information online. Technological solutions also play a crucial role. Implementing firewalls, antivirus software, and intrusion detection systems can help protect computer systems and networks from cyberattacks. Regular software updates and security patches are essential to address vulnerabilities and prevent exploitation. Cybersecurity is not just a technical issue; it requires a collaborative effort between individuals, businesses, government agencies, and law enforcement. Sharing information about cyber threats and best practices is crucial to staying ahead of the curve. Law enforcement agencies need to be equipped with the skills and resources to investigate cybercrimes, apprehend offenders, and recover stolen data. This requires specialized training, forensic tools, and collaboration with international law enforcement agencies. International cooperation is essential in combating cybercrime, as cybercriminals often operate across borders. Sharing information, coordinating investigations, and extraditing offenders are all critical to bringing cybercriminals to justice.

In conclusion, addressing specific crime types requires a tailored approach that considers the unique characteristics of each offense. A successful strategy combines proactive prevention measures, targeted enforcement efforts, and a focus on addressing the underlying causes of crime. By working together, law enforcement, community organizations, and individuals can create safer and more resilient communities. We must adapt, learn, and innovate to stay ahead of evolving criminal tactics, ensuring the safety and security of our society. The effort is ongoing, but the rewards of a safer, more just world are well worth the commitment.

6.1 Combating Violent Crime

Violent crime casts a long shadow, leaving behind shattered lives and fractured communities. It's a complex issue, deeply intertwined with social, economic, and psychological factors. Successfully combating it demands a multifaceted approach, one that goes beyond simply reacting to incidents and instead focuses on preventing them from happening in the first place. We must first understand that there is not one single magic bullet that will solve everything, but a combination of evidence-based strategies implemented consistently and adapted to local contexts. One of the most crucial elements in combating violent crime is effective community engagement. This means fostering strong relationships between law enforcement and the communities they serve. It's about building trust, encouraging open communication, and working together to identify and address the root causes of crime. When residents feel safe and trust the police, they are more likely to report suspicious activity, cooperate with investigations, and participate in crime prevention initiatives. Community engagement can take many forms, from neighborhood watch programs and community meetings to joint problem-solving initiatives that bring together residents, police officers, and other stakeholders.

The focus must shift to viewing communities not just as recipients of services, but as active partners in creating safer environments. This also requires a commitment from law enforcement to be transparent and accountable, ensuring that their actions are perceived as fair and just.

Early intervention programs are another critical component. These programs target at-risk youth, providing them with the support and resources they need to stay on the right path. This could include mentoring programs, after-school activities, educational support, and family counseling. The goal is to address the underlying factors that can lead to criminal behavior, such as poverty, lack of opportunity, and exposure to violence. For example, offering vocational training, giving people the tools to be employed is a step in the right direction to get them off the streets. These types of programs not only helps individuals, but also strengthen communities by reducing crime rates and fostering a sense of hope and opportunity.

Effective policing strategies are also essential. This includes deploying resources strategically, using data-driven approaches to identify crime hotspots, and focusing on proactive policing strategies that deter crime before it happens. It also means investing in training and technology to equip officers with the skills and tools they need to effectively investigate and solve crimes. Furthermore, building strong relationships with the community is crucial. Community policing models, where officers are assigned to specific neighborhoods and get to know the residents, can help build trust and improve communication. I have seen this being effective, however, it takes a lot of resources. Modern policing techniques emphasize de-escalation tactics, crisis intervention training, and cultural sensitivity training to ensure that officers are equipped to handle diverse situations in a safe and respectful manner.

The judicial system plays a vital role as well. Fair and impartial justice is essential for maintaining public trust and deterring crime. Sentencing guidelines should be carefully considered to ensure that punishments are proportionate to the crime and that offenders are held accountable for their actions. However, it's also important to consider alternatives to incarceration, such as community service and restorative justice programs, particularly for non-violent offenders. These programs can be more effective at reducing recidivism and helping offenders reintegrate into society. Furthermore, the judicial system should prioritize the rights of victims, ensuring that they are informed about the progress of their case and have access to support services.

Rehabilitation and reintegration programs are crucial for reducing recidivism and helping former offenders become productive members of society. These programs should provide access to vocational training, educational opportunities, and mental health services. They should also help offenders find housing and employment, addressing the barriers that can prevent them from successfully reintegrating into the community. Support systems for ex-offenders, such as mentoring programs and peer support groups, can also play a vital role.

Addressing gun violence is a critical aspect of combating violent crime.

This requires a comprehensive approach that includes strengthening gun laws, improving background checks, and investing in programs that reduce gun violence. It also means addressing the underlying factors that contribute to gun violence, such as poverty, lack of opportunity, and mental health issues. For example, focusing police efforts on areas that are experiencing high-rates of crime is a good way to approach it, and focusing on specific individuals committing crimes is another way.

The media also has a role to play. Sensationalizing violent crime can create fear and distrust, while responsible reporting can help inform the public and promote solutions. Media outlets should focus on covering the root causes of crime, highlighting effective prevention strategies, and showcasing the positive impact of community initiatives. They should also be mindful of the language they use, avoiding stereotypes and promoting empathy and understanding.

Finally, we must recognize that combating violent crime is an ongoing process that requires a long-term commitment. It requires a sustained investment in resources, a willingness to adapt strategies based on evidence, and a collaborative effort involving all stakeholders. By working together, we can create safer communities where everyone has the opportunity to thrive. It is a fight that must be fought on all fronts, with unwavering determination and a commitment to justice. The safety and well-being of our communities depend on it.

6.2 Controlling Property Crime

Property crime, though often perceived as less serious than violent offenses, erodes a community's sense of security and well-being. It can range from petty theft and vandalism to more organized operations like burglary and vehicle theft, impacting individuals and businesses alike. Effective control requires a multi-faceted approach, blending proactive prevention, targeted policing, and community involvement. We need to acknowledge that property crime is not just an economic issue; it's a social problem that demands a comprehensive response.

One crucial element is target hardening. This involves making homes, businesses, and vehicles less attractive targets for criminals. For residences, this could include installing security systems, reinforcing doors and windows, and ensuring adequate lighting. For businesses, measures like installing security cameras, employing security guards, and implementing access control systems can deter potential offenders. Public spaces can also benefit from environmental design strategies, such as improving street lighting, trimming overgrown vegetation, and increasing visibility to deter criminal activity. Furthermore, promoting community awareness campaigns that educate residents and business owners about crime prevention techniques can significantly reduce opportunities for property crime.

Another vital strategy is focused deterrence. This approach identifies high-risk individuals and groups involved in property crime and delivers a clear message about the consequences of their actions. Focused deterrence involves a combination of law enforcement efforts, social services, and community engagement to address the underlying factors contributing to their criminal behavior. For example, providing job training, educational opportunities, and drug treatment programs can help reduce recidivism among offenders. At the same time, law enforcement can use targeted patrols, surveillance, and enforcement actions to disrupt criminal networks and deter further offending. Regular meetings with offenders, law enforcement, and community leaders can also provide a platform for open communication and accountability.

Data-driven policing plays a crucial role in controlling property crime. Analyzing crime data to identify hotspots, trends, and patterns allows law enforcement agencies to allocate resources more effectively and target their efforts where they are most needed. This can involve using crime mapping software to visualize crime data, identifying repeat offenders and prolific offenders, and analyzing the types of property being targeted. Data-driven policing can also help identify underlying factors contributing to property crime, such as poverty, unemployment, and lack of access to social services. By addressing these underlying factors, law enforcement can work with community partners to develop long-term solutions to reduce crime.

Community engagement is essential for preventing and controlling property crime. Building strong relationships between law enforcement and the community can foster trust, improve communication, and encourage residents to report suspicious activity. Community watch programs, neighborhood meetings, and citizen patrols can empower residents to take an active role in crime prevention. Furthermore, community engagement can help identify and address underlying social and economic factors that contribute to property crime, such as poverty, unemployment, and lack of opportunity. By working together, law enforcement and the community can create safer and more resilient neighborhoods.

Addressing underlying social and economic factors is crucial for long-term crime prevention. Property crime is often driven by poverty, unemployment, and lack of access to social services. Investing in education, job training, and affordable housing can help reduce these underlying factors and create opportunities for individuals to lead productive lives. Providing access to mental health services and substance abuse treatment can also help address the root causes of offending. By addressing these underlying factors, communities can create a more equitable and just society that reduces the likelihood of property crime.

Technology can also play a significant role in preventing and controlling property crime. Security cameras, alarm systems, and GPS tracking devices can deter potential offenders and help recover stolen property. Social media can be used to disseminate information about crime trends, missing persons, and wanted suspects. Furthermore, law enforcement agencies can use technology to improve their response times, enhance their investigative capabilities, and analyze crime data more effectively. Embracing technological advancements can help law enforcement stay ahead of criminals and create safer communities.

Finally, effective prosecution and sentencing are essential for holding offenders accountable and deterring future crime. Prosecutors should work closely with law enforcement to build strong cases and ensure that offenders are held responsible for their actions. Sentencing guidelines should be fair and consistent, taking into account the severity of the crime, the offender's criminal history, and the impact on the victim. Alternatives to incarceration, such as probation, community service, and restorative justice programs, can be effective for lower-level property offenses, particularly for first-time offenders. However, repeat offenders and those involved in more serious property crimes should face appropriate penalties, including imprisonment, to deter future offending and protect the community.

6.3 Cybercrime Prevention and Response

Cybercrime is a pervasive and rapidly evolving threat, demanding a comprehensive and adaptive approach to prevention and response. Its borderless nature, coupled with the increasing sophistication of cybercriminals, makes it a particularly challenging area for law enforcement and cybersecurity professionals. The financial losses and personal data breaches resulting from cyberattacks can have a devastating impact on individuals, businesses, and even critical infrastructure.

Effective cybercrime prevention begins with a strong foundation of awareness and education. Individuals need to be equipped with the knowledge and skills to identify potential threats and avoid falling victim to common scams and phishing attacks. This includes understanding the importance of strong passwords, being cautious about clicking on suspicious links or attachments, and regularly updating software to patch security vulnerabilities. Businesses, too, must prioritize cybersecurity awareness training for their employees, emphasizing the potential risks associated with social engineering tactics and the need to adhere to strict data security protocols. Moreover, public awareness campaigns can play a crucial role in educating the broader population about emerging cyber threats and best practices for online safety.

Beyond individual and organizational awareness, proactive cybersecurity measures are essential to mitigate the risk of cyberattacks. Implementing robust firewalls, intrusion detection systems, and anti-malware software can help to prevent unauthorized access to computer systems and networks. Regular security audits and vulnerability assessments can identify weaknesses in an organization's infrastructure and allow for timely remediation. Data encryption is another critical security measure, protecting sensitive information from being accessed or stolen in the event of a breach. Furthermore, businesses should implement a comprehensive data backup and recovery plan to ensure that they can quickly restore their operations in the event of a ransomware attack or other data loss incident. Collaboration and information sharing between organizations and law enforcement agencies are also vital for staying ahead of evolving cyber threats.

When a cybercrime incident does occur, a swift and coordinated response is critical to minimizing the damage and bringing the perpetrators to justice. The first step is to immediately contain the incident, isolating affected systems and preventing further spread of the attack. A thorough investigation should then be conducted to determine the scope of the breach, identify the vulnerabilities that were exploited, and gather evidence for potential prosecution. Law enforcement agencies should be notified as soon as possible, particularly in cases involving serious crimes such as data theft, fraud, or extortion. Working with cybersecurity experts can help to ensure that the investigation is conducted effectively and that all relevant evidence is preserved. Finally, it is essential to provide timely and accurate information to affected individuals and stakeholders, keeping them informed about the incident and the steps being taken to address it.

International cooperation is essential in combating cybercrime, given its transnational nature. Cybercriminals often operate from different countries, making it difficult to track them down and bring them to justice. Strengthening international partnerships and collaboration between law enforcement agencies can help to overcome these challenges. This includes sharing intelligence about cyber threats, coordinating investigations, and extraditing cybercriminals to face prosecution. Harmonizing cybercrime laws and regulations across different jurisdictions can also facilitate international cooperation and ensure that cybercriminals are held accountable for their actions. Furthermore, international organizations like the United Nations and the Council of Europe play a crucial role in promoting international cooperation and developing international standards for cybercrime prevention and response.

Adapting to the evolving threat landscape requires ongoing research and development in cybersecurity technologies and techniques. This includes developing new methods for detecting and preventing cyberattacks, improving data encryption and security protocols, and enhancing the resilience of critical infrastructure. Investing in cybersecurity education and training is also essential to ensure that there is a sufficient pool of skilled professionals to address the growing demand for cybersecurity expertise. Collaboration between academia, industry, and government is crucial for fostering innovation and developing effective solutions to the challenges posed by cybercrime. Furthermore, ethical considerations should be at the forefront of cybersecurity research and development, ensuring that new technologies are used responsibly and do not infringe on individual rights or freedoms.

Legal frameworks play a vital role in establishing clear rules and regulations for cyberspace and holding cybercriminals accountable for their actions. Cybercrime laws should be comprehensive and adaptable, covering a wide range of offenses, including hacking, data theft, fraud, and online harassment. These laws should also provide law enforcement agencies with the necessary powers to investigate and prosecute cybercrimes effectively. Furthermore, international treaties and agreements can help to harmonize cybercrime laws across different jurisdictions and facilitate international cooperation. However, it is essential to ensure that cybercrime laws are balanced and do not unduly restrict freedom of expression or other fundamental rights. Legal frameworks should also address issues such as data privacy, cybersecurity standards, and liability for cyberattacks.

Community involvement is a critical component of cybercrime prevention and response. Encouraging individuals and organizations to report cybercrime incidents can help to provide a more accurate picture of the threat landscape and enable law enforcement agencies to take appropriate action. Community watch programs can also be adapted to address cybercrime, educating residents about common scams and phishing attacks and encouraging them to report suspicious activity. Furthermore, partnerships between law enforcement agencies and community organizations can help to build trust and improve communication, leading to more effective cybercrime prevention and response efforts. Empowering individuals and communities to take ownership of their cybersecurity can significantly reduce the risk of cybercrime and create a safer online environment.

7 Chapter 7: Maintaining Societal Stability

Maintaining societal stability in the face of criminal conduct requires a multi-faceted approach, one that goes beyond simply reacting to crime after it has occurred. It demands proactive measures that foster trust in institutions and promote social cohesion. These elements are not merely desirable; they are essential pillars upon which a stable and well-functioning society is built. Without them, even the most effective law enforcement and judicial systems will struggle to maintain order and prevent the erosion of public confidence. Trust, in this context, isn't a passive acceptance; it's an earned commodity, cultivated through transparency, accountability, and consistent delivery of justice. This trust becomes a social capital, readily available for institutions to manage conduct violations restoring societal calm and stability.

One of the primary ways to build trust in institutions is through consistent and transparent communication. Agencies need to be open about their operations, policies, and performance. This includes making data available to the public, holding regular town hall meetings, and responding promptly and thoroughly to inquiries from the media and the public. When institutions operate in secrecy, suspicion and mistrust inevitably fester. For example, law enforcement agencies should regularly publish crime statistics, use-of-force data, and information about disciplinary actions taken against officers. The judicial system should ensure that court proceedings are open to the public and that legal documents are easily accessible. Government agencies should be transparent about their spending and decision-making processes. Of course, there are legitimate reasons for confidentiality in certain situations, such as protecting ongoing investigations or sensitive personal information. However, these exceptions should be clearly defined and narrowly applied, with a presumption in favor of transparency. If this is done, institutions can have a better image in the eyes of the community and can work better.

Accountability is another crucial component of building trust. Institutions must be held responsible for their actions, and individuals within those institutions must be held accountable for their misconduct. This requires clear lines of authority, robust oversight mechanisms, and effective disciplinary procedures. Law enforcement agencies should have independent oversight boards to investigate complaints of police misconduct. The judicial system should have mechanisms for reviewing judicial decisions and disciplining judges who violate ethical standards. Government agencies should have internal audit departments to identify and prevent waste, fraud, and abuse. Crucially, accountability must be applied fairly and consistently, regardless of rank or position. When people see that those in power are not held to the same standards as everyone else, it erodes trust in the entire system. Institutions are often the cornerstone of civilization, and maintaining an image that will give confidence to the citizens can only mean a more healthy society.

Beyond transparency and accountability, institutions must also demonstrate their commitment to fairness and justice. This means ensuring that everyone is treated equally under the law, regardless of their race, ethnicity, religion, gender, or socioeconomic status. It also means addressing systemic inequalities that may contribute to crime and social unrest. For instance, law enforcement agencies should implement training programs to address implicit bias and promote cultural sensitivity. The judicial system should work to eliminate racial disparities in sentencing. Government agencies should invest in programs that promote economic opportunity in disadvantaged communities. The key is to show that institutions are not only committed to enforcing the law but also to creating a more just and equitable society for all. This work will always be difficult. There are a lot of social issues that need to be addressed to achieve such thing, but it will be worthwhile.

Promoting social cohesion is equally important for maintaining societal stability. Social cohesion refers to the bonds that unite people within a community and enable them to work together for the common good. It is characterized by a sense of shared identity, mutual respect, and a willingness to cooperate. When social cohesion is strong, people are more likely to trust each other, support their neighbors, and participate in civic life. This, in turn, reduces crime, strengthens communities, and promotes overall well-being. Social cohesion allows for people to be in harmony and to be open minded to the possibility of forming strong relationships with others. When relationships are stable, there is less possibility of conflict and more chances for communities to grow.

One way to promote social cohesion is to foster a sense of shared identity. This can be done through public education campaigns that celebrate the diversity of the community, promote understanding of different cultures, and highlight the values that unite people. Schools can play a crucial role in teaching students about their shared history and promoting civic engagement. Community events, such as festivals, parades, and sporting events, can also bring people together and foster a sense of belonging. Encouraging intergroup dialogue and collaboration is a huge step forward in social cohesion. It is possible to have different backgrounds but come to a mutual understanding.

Another way to promote social cohesion is to encourage volunteerism and civic participation. When people get involved in their communities, they develop a stronger sense of connection to others and a greater stake in the well-being of their neighborhoods. This can take many forms, from volunteering at a local food bank to serving on a community board to participating in a neighborhood watch program. The key is to provide opportunities for people to contribute to their communities and to feel like they are making a difference. If more people feel they belong to something bigger than themselves, they will feel the need to fight for that and keep it safe.

Addressing economic inequality is also crucial for promoting social cohesion. When there is a wide gap between the rich and the poor, it can create resentment and division. People who feel marginalized and excluded are more likely to turn to crime and violence. Therefore, it is important to invest in programs that promote economic opportunity for all, such as job training, affordable housing, and access to healthcare. It is also important to ensure that everyone has access to a quality education, regardless of their socioeconomic background. A level playing field is essential for building a cohesive and equitable society. This could mean better resources for the less fortunate or a reform in taxes, making it so everyone pays their fair share.

Finally, it is important to promote respectful dialogue and understanding across different groups. In today's society, there are often deep divisions along racial, ethnic, religious, and political lines. These divisions can lead to polarization, conflict, and even violence. Therefore, it is important to create opportunities for people to come together and engage in respectful dialogue about difficult issues. This can be done through community forums, interfaith gatherings, and educational programs. The goal is to promote understanding, empathy, and a willingness to compromise. If people can learn to listen to each other and see the world from different perspectives, they are more likely to find common ground and work together for the common good. This can only result in a more cohesive and developed society.

7.1 Building Trust in Institutions

Trust in institutions is the bedrock of a stable society, and when it erodes, the consequences are far-reaching, impacting everything from compliance with laws to participation in civic life. Rebuilding and maintaining that trust requires a multifaceted approach, focusing on transparency, accountability, responsiveness, and demonstrable fairness. It is not simply about public relations; it demands genuine reform and a commitment to ethical conduct at all levels.

One crucial step is enhancing transparency. This means making information readily available to the public regarding policies, procedures, and decision-making processes. Law enforcement agencies, for example, can publish data on arrest rates, use of force incidents, and complaint statistics. Courts can offer clear explanations of legal proceedings and sentencing guidelines. Government agencies can disclose details about budgets, contracts, and performance metrics. The goal is to eliminate the perception of secrecy and foster a sense of openness, which in turn breeds trust. This transparency must also extend to admitting mistakes. When errors occur, institutions must acknowledge them openly, take responsibility, and outline the steps they are taking to prevent recurrence. Hiding or downplaying errors only serves to further erode public confidence. Consider the impact of a police department that readily admits to procedural errors in a high-profile case, compared to one that attempts to cover them up. The former, while facing initial criticism, ultimately demonstrates a commitment to justice that can enhance long-term trust. Accountability mechanisms are equally critical. Institutions must establish clear channels for citizens to voice their concerns and hold them responsible for their actions. Independent oversight bodies, such as civilian review boards for police departments, can provide a neutral platform for investigating complaints and recommending disciplinary action. Judicial review processes ensure that government decisions are subject to scrutiny and can be challenged in court. Whistleblower protection laws encourage individuals to report misconduct without fear of retaliation. Furthermore, accountability must extend to all levels of an organization, from frontline employees to senior leaders. Leaders must be held responsible for creating a culture of ethics and ensuring that policies are consistently enforced. This might involve performance evaluations that include measures of ethical conduct, or disciplinary action for those who violate established standards.

Responsiveness is another key element. Institutions must demonstrate that they are responsive to the needs and concerns of the communities they serve. This means actively seeking input from the public, engaging in dialogue, and adapting policies and practices based on feedback. Town hall meetings, community surveys, and online forums can provide valuable opportunities for citizens to share their perspectives and hold institutions accountable. Responsiveness also requires providing timely and accurate information in response to inquiries from the public. Delays, evasiveness, or a lack of clarity can create suspicion and undermine trust. Public services should strive to be user-friendly and accessible, with clear lines of communication and efficient processes for resolving issues. Beyond these specific measures, a fundamental shift in mindset is often necessary. Institutions must move away from a top-down, authoritarian approach and embrace a more collaborative, community-oriented model. This means recognizing that citizens are not simply passive recipients of services, but active partners in creating a safer and more just society. Law enforcement agencies, for example, can work with community organizations to develop crime prevention strategies that are tailored to local needs. Courts can implement restorative justice programs that bring offenders and victims together to address the harm caused by crime. Government agencies can empower citizens to participate in decision-making processes through participatory budgeting and community planning initiatives.

Fairness is essential for building and maintaining trust. The perception of bias or discrimination can quickly undermine public confidence in institutions. It is crucial that policies and practices are applied equitably to all individuals, regardless of their race, ethnicity, religion, or socioeconomic status. This requires addressing systemic biases that may exist within institutions and implementing measures to promote diversity and inclusion. Law enforcement agencies, for example, can implement implicit bias training for officers and diversify their recruitment efforts to better reflect the communities they serve. Courts can monitor sentencing outcomes to identify and address disparities based on race or ethnicity. Furthermore, institutions must be willing to acknowledge and address past injustices. Ignoring or downplaying historical wrongs can perpetuate distrust and resentment. Truth and reconciliation commissions, apologies, and reparations can be important steps in acknowledging past harms and promoting healing. For example, a police department that acknowledges its history of discriminatory practices and implements reforms to address them can begin to rebuild trust with marginalized communities. However, these efforts must be genuine and sustained. Token gestures or superficial reforms will not suffice. The commitment to fairness must be embedded in the culture of the institution and demonstrated through consistent actions.

Ultimately, building trust in institutions is a long-term process that requires sustained effort and a genuine commitment to ethical conduct. There are no quick fixes or easy solutions. It demands a willingness to listen, learn, and adapt, as well as a recognition that institutions are accountable to the people they serve. By embracing transparency, accountability, responsiveness, and fairness, institutions can begin to rebuild public confidence and create a more just and stable society. This proactive and continuous approach is essential to foster long-term societal stability and effectively control criminal elements. The reward for such efforts is a citizenry that is more willing to cooperate with authorities, abide by the law, and participate in the democratic process, leading to a safer and more harmonious society for all.

7.2 Promoting Social Cohesion

Social cohesion is the glue that binds a community together, and without it, any efforts to control crime are ultimately weakened. It's the shared values, the mutual trust, and the sense of belonging that empower individuals to look out for one another and collectively address issues like criminal conduct. Building this cohesion is not a passive process; it demands deliberate and sustained effort from all stakeholders – residents, community organizations, law enforcement, and local government. I believe that fostering a society where individuals feel connected and responsible for each other is essential to preventing and addressing criminal behavior.

One of the most potent tools for promoting social cohesion is strengthening community bonds. This can be achieved through various initiatives that encourage interaction and cooperation among residents. Think about neighborhood associations, community gardens, local festivals, and shared spaces where people can connect, interact and build relationships. These spaces and activities provide opportunities for individuals from diverse backgrounds to come together, share experiences, and develop a sense of shared identity. I see firsthand how successful communities invest in creating these opportunities. Another crucial element is promoting intergenerational engagement. Programs that connect older adults with youth, such as mentoring programs or joint community service projects, can foster understanding and respect between generations, as well as transmit valuable knowledge and skills. By creating platforms for meaningful interaction, we can break down social barriers and build a stronger sense of community.

Addressing inequalities is fundamental to promoting social cohesion. When significant disparities exist in access to resources, opportunities, and justice, it erodes trust and fuels resentment, creating an environment ripe for crime. Initiatives aimed at reducing poverty, improving education, expanding access to healthcare, and promoting affordable housing are essential for creating a more equitable society. Furthermore, it's crucial to address systemic discrimination and bias that disproportionately affect certain groups. Promoting diversity and inclusion in all aspects of community life, from education and employment to housing and governance, is vital for ensuring that everyone feels valued and has the opportunity to thrive. My personal experience shows that inclusive communities are more resilient and less susceptible to crime.

Another important aspect is to encourage civic engagement and participation. When residents feel that they have a voice in shaping their community and are empowered to participate in decision-making processes, they are more likely to invest in its well-being. This can be achieved through town hall meetings, community forums, neighborhood councils, and participatory budgeting initiatives. It's also important to ensure that all residents, including marginalized groups, have access to information and resources necessary to participate effectively in civic life. By empowering residents to become active stakeholders in their communities, we can create a stronger sense of ownership and collective responsibility. This, in turn, will help to foster greater social cohesion and reduce the likelihood of criminal conduct.

Rebuilding trust in institutions, particularly law enforcement and the justice system, is critical. Unfortunately, negative interactions or perceived biases can erode public trust and create a sense of alienation, especially among marginalized communities. To rebuild trust, it's essential for institutions to be transparent, accountable, and responsive to community concerns. This includes implementing policies that promote fairness and impartiality, providing training to personnel on cultural sensitivity and de-escalation techniques, and establishing independent oversight mechanisms to investigate complaints of misconduct. Moreover, fostering positive relationships between law enforcement and the community through community policing initiatives and regular dialogue can help bridge the gap and build mutual understanding. I learned that trust is the cornerstone of effective crime prevention and control.

Promoting restorative justice practices offers a powerful way to address crime and repair harm in a way that strengthens social cohesion. Unlike traditional punitive approaches, restorative justice focuses on bringing together victims, offenders, and community members to address the harm caused by a crime and develop a plan for repairing the damage. This process can help victims heal from their trauma, hold offenders accountable for their actions, and promote reconciliation between offenders and the community. By emphasizing dialogue, empathy, and accountability, restorative justice can foster a sense of shared responsibility and help to rebuild trust and social cohesion. It's not always an easy path, but the results can be transformative.

Education and awareness campaigns play a vital role in promoting social cohesion by challenging stereotypes, promoting understanding, and fostering empathy. These campaigns can address a wide range of issues, such as cultural diversity, tolerance, conflict resolution, and the root causes of crime. Utilizing various media platforms, community events, and educational programs can disseminate information, share personal stories, and create opportunities for dialogue and reflection. It is my understanding that effective education and awareness campaigns can help to dismantle prejudice, build bridges between different groups, and promote a more inclusive and cohesive society.

Creating opportunities for cross-cultural understanding and dialogue can break down barriers and foster empathy. Organizing cultural exchange programs, community dialogues, and interfaith events can help people learn about different cultures, perspectives, and experiences. These opportunities can challenge stereotypes, promote understanding, and build relationships across cultural divides. Furthermore, supporting language learning programs and cultural arts initiatives can help to preserve and celebrate the diversity within a community. When people have the opportunity to connect with others who are different from them, it expands their horizons and fosters a greater sense of belonging.

Ultimately, promoting social cohesion requires a multifaceted approach that addresses the underlying causes of crime and fosters a sense of community, trust, and shared responsibility. By strengthening community bonds, addressing inequalities, encouraging civic engagement, rebuilding trust in institutions, promoting restorative justice practices, implementing education and awareness campaigns, and creating opportunities for cross-cultural understanding, we can build a society that is more resilient, just, and peaceful. It's a long-term investment, but one that yields immeasurable returns in terms of societal well-being and stability. I firmly believe that a cohesive society is a safer society.

www.ingramcontent.com/pod-product-compliance
Lightning Source LLC
LaVergne TN
LVHW022232200926
848481LV00006B/2233
* 9 7 9 8 8 6 9 0 4 3 2 5 2 *